"Learning from Justin has been just what I needed! If I had his tactics from the beginning of my business, I know I would have already attained an extra rank—maybe even two! His tactics help you know how to draw out the best in you, while finding the areas you need help in!"

Lori Borre

"I wanted to market my business using social media, but I had no clue where to begin. Justin's tactics on Facebook classes were just what I needed! They walked me step-by-step through the process of a successful Facebook class. First, I needed to understand the theory behind this type of class and then I needed to gain confidence in my efforts.

Through these tactics and the appropriate resources, I created unique content and graphics for my class. The result was a positive, upbeat, unique, and a well-attended class. He has a working knowledge of successful Facebook classes with a unique approach and fresh ideas. I found the experience challenging yet positive, definitely a growth experience and a move in the right direction. I would recommend Justin and his teachings to others who want to expand their business into the social media world."

Amy Hineman

"Applying the concepts taught by Justin is a breath of fresh air. He teaches and gives you tools to grow your business and the confidence to do it. He reiterates over and over again to keep working hard, but I know he believes I can see success."

Sally Wilson

The SUMMIT

A Network Marketer's Guide to the Top

JUSTIN PITTS

The Summit

Visit **facebook.com/trainwithjustin** for information on additional copies, trainings, events, and more.

Edited by Jonathan Timothy
Formatting and Layout by Jonathan Timothy

ISBN: 978-1546437390

First Edition: June 2017

Dedication

This book is dedicated to those of you who have ever been beat down when attempting to accomplish your goals, to those individuals that believe in you, and to each of you reading this book!

I remember being in 8th grade and having a teacher tell me that I would never do anything productive, or be successful at anything in life. That experience motivated me—even more than I was before—to make my dreams happen and to experience success. Since that experience, I have learned so much and have become a better person. I write this book because we all have people in our lives who try to get us down, who tell us we can't do something, and who try to persuade us from accomplishing our dreams. Sadly these people will always show up, so decide not to let them get you down or stop you from making things happen.

I want you to know that I believe in you and know you can do this! There are going to be hard times—and it will take work—but you have just what it takes to become a success and make your dreams a reality. I am so thankful for my parents, grandparents, friends, and family who have always pushed and encouraged me to be the very best version of myself. When time gets tough or others try to get you down, focus on those that are there to support and help you make it. Find those that believe in you, believe in yourself, and you will make your dreams a reality!

I am in your corner, rooting you on every step of the way!

Contents

Introduction

To be perfectly honest with you, I never saw myself writing a book or being in the position where I would be helping thousands of people grow successful businesses. However, at times, life guides us down paths and puts us in positions where we can help others. Personally, I've always had a passion for helping others, seeing them succeed, and providing proven resources to experience success. Like many of you, I have read scores of books on the market and taken time to apply the principles, but I found myself getting discouraged and frustrated. As great as some of these books and tools claimed to be, many of them have a deficit of detail or provide outdated methods that expect you to try to implement into our modern world.

However, it is so important to adapt in our industry with the changes caused by modern technology, the evolution of the Internet, the rise of social media, and changes within the minds of consumers. Let's face it, times have changed drastically even within the last 15-20 years! In order to adapt to these changes, our approach and tactics need to change. I realized that part of my frustrations and discouragement with the other books were caused by two main reasons:

1. The lack of addressing the changes of modern technology, the evolution of the Internet, the rise of social media, and changes within the minds of consumers.

2. They provided "feel good" fluff and more theory behind concepts instead of teaching practical, step-by-step guidelines needed to help you succeed.

The Summit is all about a new approach that works. It teaches not only the concepts behind foundational, network marketing principles, but it also provides step-by-step examples, outlines, and guidelines about what you need to do to experience success in this industry. Consider the analogy of making it to the summit of one of the world's largest mountains. Many dream about reaching the tops of these magnificent peaks—to take in the majestic vistas, to experience the rewarding feeling that they made it to the top, and to celebrate the lifetime achievement with others. However, how many actually make it to the summit?

Forget the summit for a moment. How many even make it outside of their own home, onto a plane, and to the base of that mountain? Here's a hint—not many in comparison to how many dream about it. In fact, a large majority of people that dream of accomplishing that ascent, never allow their dream to leave the confines of their own minds. Similar to this situation, how many individuals get into this industry with this same thought process? They have lofty goals of making it to the summit of success—whether that be to reach a certain rank, achieve financial freedom, earn a specific amount of income, or any number of other goals—but don't even get close to it.

This reality can be caused from a number of reasons including insufficient training, laziness, false expectations, little or no support, the lack of proper tools, minimal or no guidance, or a slew of other reasons. Whatever your reason is (or reasons are), you need to take control of your own destiny and address what you can control. This book was designed with these circumstances in mind. It doesn't matter if you don't have supportive leaders, if you don't know where to begin, or if you lack knowledge about your company, products, or services. You can reach the goals that you want to reach by using the hands-on tactics this book provides—no matter where you are at in your business or how long you've been doing it.

Think back to our summit analogy. For those individuals who actually reached the mountain to climb, how many of them did it alone? How many of them did it without a plan? Without tools? Without a guide? Successful mountain climbers adequately prepare by having the necessary tools, plans, and guides to help them reach the summit. That's exactly what this book is going to do! It will provide you with the necessary tools, plans, and guides you need to reach the summit of success in this industry and make network marketing a viable and thriving way to earn an income.

Just like the experienced Himalayan mountain guides, consider me as your literary guide on this journey. Of course scaling a mountain takes hard work, preparation, and determination—so I ask that you commit to applying these as you read this book. I will help eliminate some of the common excuses that are rampant in our industry. As you do this and follow the suggestions and hands-on tactics, you will see results. A word of caution though.

At times you will experience individuals or groups who want to discourage you on this journey. Be aware that these naysayers will likely cross your path. They will try (and sometimes succeed) to beat you down, tell you that you can't succeed, that your products or services aren't worth it, that the industry isn't legitimate, or even that you can't be successful if you didn't get into your company at the very beginning. Don't listen to these negative voices or let them derail your efforts. I will provide you with the necessary tools for you to succeed, but even more important than that, you will need to have determination and believe in yourself. You can do this!

Sometimes we end up in places we never could have imagined we'd be in and that is both scary and exciting at the same time! Network marketing can be much like this description—both scary and exciting. It can also be very rewarding and financially beneficial. Focus on the positive and do your best to implement the tactics, suggestions, and guidelines in each chapter. Of course, it will take time to master everything (I'm still working on some of these things too), but each of the tactics are proven methods that I've personally used and coached on.

Most people in the industry start because they see the vision, they catch the excitement, they love a company's products or services, but they simply lack the know-how to make it happen. Don't let this happen to you. Oftentimes, we also feel alone in our efforts—and sometimes that is true. However, you don't have to go at it alone anymore. As I look at my time in this industry as a coach, network marketer, and manager on the corporate side—and what motivates me—it's all about helping individuals succeed. Oftentimes training and education is not available to all those that need it. The goal of this book is to provide quality training and to give everyone the chance to succeed. In part, I created this book so I could live my "why" by sharing my knowledge and experiences to a much larger audience in order to help them improve and succeed at their businesses.

You don't have to start or fair the journey alone—together let's begin our ascent to reaching the summit!

How to Use this Book

This book has been divided into seven chapters, which represent some of the most important, foundational topics and tactics you need to know to succeed in your efforts. I tried to lay it out so each chapter builds upon the previous one. However, some of the material can and should be implemented at the same time. Each chapter will contain a loose narrative coupled with hands-on activities, examples, and guidelines. Unfortunately, book format does not allow me to cater the content directly to your company. However, the information included is sound and can be applied across all different types of companies within the Network Marketing industry.

Instead of providing a list of tips and references at the end of each chapter, I have placed them directly within the text throughout the book. Tips will give you helpful information and suggestions directly where it applies within the text and references will direct you to other chapters in the book where you can learn more or remind you about a topic covered in the book. Both the tip and reference boxes have recognizable symbols in the upper left corner (a compass for Tips and a book for References), to help you visually identify them as well as understand what type of information you will be receiving. They will look like this:

> **Tip:** You can't be detailed enough in Step 6 of the Marketing Plan. If you're able to break it down into monthly, weekly, or even daily goals this will ensure you accomplish your overall goals.

> **Reference:** Please see the Prospecting chapter of this book for creative ways to find new people and to start the 60-day Prospecting Plan.

Additionally, I have included a To Do List and a Chapter Notes section at the end of every chapter. The To Do List provides some high level takeaways from that particular chapter and will allow you to check them off as you incorporate them into your efforts. The Chapter Notes section provides you with a place to write down notes if needed.

Terminology

Throughout the book, I use a handful of industry-related terms and phrases that may or may not fit your particular definition. I have equipped you with a list of terms or phrases—and my associated definitions of them—in order to provide better clarity about exactly what I mean when I use them. I recognize that some of these can be perceived or defined differently than my usage, but I hope that these definitions will offer perspective and the intended meaning as you read The Summit.

Products or Services - This book has been designed for all network marketers, from all different types of companies. Some companies have products, while others offer services. In order to accommodate for all of these, I use the term "products or services" many times throughout this book. Obviously I want you to identify with the term that best suits your situation.

Prospects - Prospects are any individuals that are not currently involved in your business.

Customers - Customers are members of your team that use your company's products or services, but are not interested in building the business.

Business Builders - Business builders use your company's products or services and also take advantage of the business opportunity.

Team - A team consists of both your customers and business builders.

Prospecting Outline - Scripts are things of the past! An outline is a series of talking points to keep with you when learning and mastering the art of prospecting.

Downline - Anyone on your team placed under you. Someone you have on your team.

Upline - The person directly above you.

Booklet - In addition to this book, I have also created a companion booklet designed to provide the first steps to help you and your business builders get their businesses going. The First Steps to the Summit booklet is a great resource that corresponds with topics covered in this book (including Self Development, Marketing, Prospecting, Sales, Classes, Education, and Leadership) and presents them in a more digestible format. This booklet can be used in your classes, while training your business builders, or to help you get started if you are new to the industry. Use both the booklet and this book to get you and your business builders started growing your businesses from day one and to be empowered with more in-depth information to continue that growth.

As you're reading, get involved and actively learn and apply the principles found in this book. Don't let this become like any other book that gets read and put on the back shelf! Use it again and again, share it, and really grow your business from it. The concepts found here are proven to work and will have a huge impact on your business. It's time to start on our journey!

Chapter 1
Self Development

If you're reading this book, then it's likely that you are in need of some additional help with your business—and you're in the right place! But before we get into some specific, hands-on tactics to apply to your business efforts, I want you to think about where you are as an individual. Are you where you want to be? Maybe you are, or maybe you aren't, but regardless of where you are currently, it's important to be open to developing yourself into someone better than you are now as well as being open to make changes to see amazing results. The first step of this journey to the summit of success starts directly with you as an individual—so let's get started.

Self Belief

Do you truly believe in yourself and your ability to succeed? I mean really believe that you can be one of the best? Oftentimes we tell ourselves we believe, that we can succeed, and that we can make it to the top of the summit. However, as I have worked with people like you in the industry, I have come to realize that many times this is simply not the case. Believing in yourself is the first step to becoming successful. It will set a foundation that you can build upon and keep momentum moving forward in your efforts to run a successful business. Once you truly realize your internal abilities and believe in yourself, nothing will be able stop you.

As a child what did you dream about becoming when you got older? What did you hope to accomplish in your life? When I was a child, I wanted to be an astronaut, a scientist, a doctor, the President of the United States, and everything in between. I wanted to travel the world learning and understanding different cultures, really experiencing what they had to offer. I wanted to be someone important and do something that no one had ever done before. The kid version of me was determined that I would make a difference, that I would be a person of power that could influence the world for good—and that I could achieve whatever I set out to accomplish. Does this sound familiar?

I'm not exactly sure when my thoughts changed, but at some point reality kicked in—and I'm sure many of you can relate. Life started to beat me down bit by bit and my childhood goals and ambitions changed. I found that experiences can sometimes serve up some disappointment or introduce fear into our lives. However, to dispel disappointment and fear, we must have the drive, ambition, and eagerness of a child. Take a few minutes to think about your childhood. What did you want to accomplish? Who did you want to become? What were you going to conquer? Can you imagine how successful you would be if you were able to harvest even a portion of that eagerness from your childhood and apply it into your daily life and business?

I love the industry we are in because it empowers individuals from all walks of life and unites them in a common cause. I love seeing people find their childhood passion and belief in themselves—after all that's what life's all about! Take some time and commit to believing a bit more in yourself, dreaming a bit bigger, and tapping into those childhood dreams you once had. Even if you didn't have lofty dreams as a child, there is a powerful potential inside each of us to excel and succeed. Once you truly believe this and you can see yourself reaching your end goal, nothing will be able to stop you. Work hard, commit today, and dream big! Now that you've tapped into this power, it is important to know how that relates to you at this point in your life and business. You've got to know your "why".

> **Tip:** Set a timer for three minutes and make a list of some of your best qualities, passions, and attributes. Ask a few of your closest friends to do the same exercise about you. Take time to compare your answers and to focus on the positive things you bring to the table. When times get tough and you struggle to believe in yourself, come back to this list and activity often. Remembering all of your qualities, passions, and attributes will help boost your confidence and help you move forward with self belief.

Know Your Why

How many times have you read a book, been to a conference, or listened to a speaker that has asked, "What is your why?" The first time I heard someone ask me this, I was fifteen-years old and I seriously started laughing. I really did not understand the big hype of needing a "why" or why it was even important. When I first heard about the "why" concept, I was sitting in Orlando, Florida, at a Disney convention. Someone was talking about their company and how they needed to have a reason why they were participating in this organization. They said not only did I need to have a "why", but that my "why" needed to make me cry, make me move others, and make me feel constantly emotional—and a handful of other wild ideas. I honestly thought they were crazy!

It seemed weird listening to a grown man tell me what reasoning I needed to have in order to be successful and exactly how I had to feel. However, I have come to realize the importance of the "why" through my experience in network marketing for over a decade, as well as coaching and mentoring others—and it isn't quite the exact way that man described it years ago, but it is an integral part of longevity and success for you and your business. And since no one likes to be told what they have to do to be a success, allow me to make a few suggestions that will help you along this journey.

First and foremost, I have realized that we all need to have something that motivates us. Think about what makes you passionate, excited, and motivated in life. For some this could be owning or driving that hot red roadster they've wanted since sixteen-years old, it could be spending more quality time with their family, it could be building an orphanage in a third-world country, or it could be traveling to an exotic location. It will be different for every individual and there is no specific motivation that your "why" has to be. However, you will need this as a foundation to build upon and support you through the hard times. And if you keep moving forward, you will hit your goals and make it to the top. Knowing and living your "why" is important, so it must be all about you!

When I think of my "why" and what motivates me, my list has a lot of items on it. Honestly, my reasons change from time to time. Depending on what is going on in my life and what is going on in the lives of others around me, my motivations change—and that's ok because it is my "why"! At the end of the day I am motivated because I love seeing people happy, I love seeing dreams become a reality, I love helping my family and friends, and I love having fun. Life is too short to not enjoy it with the people we love and cherish. That is what motivates me on the hard days and keeps me going when I want to quit. And no matter what others think, it's what makes me happy.

Now really think about your "why" and what it is that makes you excited. Think about why you do what you do and what will keep you going when times get tough. Think about how you're going to enjoy your "why" and live it the way you have always dreamed would make you the most happy.

Don't wait to live your "why"—start now! Find ways you can put your "why" into practice, or ways you can start living the life you want. It may have to be in small steps, but that's ok. For example, a member in my downline is motivated by traveling to exotic locations. However, she doesn't have the financial means to reach all of those places on her list, so she has started to budget for some smaller trips. These trips continue to motivate her and push her through the hard times, so one day she can reach those exotic locations. So set your "why", stay focused, and be prepared to work. No matter how challenging things get, how tight money might be, or how hard life is, remember your "why" and don't give up.

> **Tip:** Once you know your "why", be sure to share it! Let others know why it's important to you, what motivates you, etc. Sharing your "why" with your team will help you develop harder working and better motivated business builders as well as more loyal customers.

Identify Strengths and Weaknesses

I've had the opportunity to work for several network marketing companies—large and small—in both the corporate offices and on the network marketing side. These experiences have expanded my abilities and given me opportunities to learn new skills. One of the greatest lessons that I've learned while being in this industry is that it will challenge you in ways you can't imagine. At times you have to be a salesperson, a marketer, an expert, a leader, an educator, a speaker, a mentor, or a number of other roles. But each of these roles allows you to use or develop skills you had no idea you possessed. And you'll be forced to find out quickly where your strengths and weaknesses lie.

It is very important you know exactly what you're good at, what areas you excel in, and what skills you can bring to the table to benefit your business builders, your customers, and your business. However, it is also equally as important for you to understand what your weaknesses are or where you need improvement. This can be very difficult for most of us and I was no exception! I "knew" I was good at everything—or if I wasn't, I could figure it out. By understanding your weaknesses, it gives you an opportunity to identify both business builders and customers that can contribute their strengths where you are lacking.

Take for example, two reputable co-founders in recent history— Steve Jobs and Steve Wozniak. I'm sure a few of you have heard of the company they created known as Apple. Each of these men were strong in their respective fields. Wozniak was a genius engineer who just wanted to build computers and was in no way a businessman. He lacked the ideas to grow a successful brand of his own. On the other hand, Steve Jobs was a visionary, who saw great potential in marketing and selling the computers Wozniak built. Like Wozniak, he also had his weaknesses and needed someone to just get the job done. Together, with each of their strengths, they were able to make one of the most successful companies in recent history.

Do you see the value of identifying not only your strengths, but also the strengths of those around you? Think about all of the skills and qualities that you need to be successful in your efforts. You need people skills, relationship skills, teaching skills, public speaking skills, patience (still something I am working on), business drive, creativity, networking, and the list seriously goes on and on. Now I want it to be very clear that if you don't have all of these skills or qualities, or if your personality pushes you in the opposite direction of some of them, don't stress. Everyone on the team can help make you a success. By their strengths they can help improve your weaknesses.

> **Tip:** Create a list of your top five strengths and weaknesses. Do this with your customers and business builders. This will help you get to know them, and also know who to rely on when you need help with something you may not be so good at. Your customers may not be interested in building the business just yet—and that's ok—but still get to know them and call on them if you ever need assistance. A new customer may not be comfortable with this at first, so only do this when it's natural and seems appropriate. This is a great way to build a solid, trusting relationship with both business builders and customers.

Identify both your strengths and weakness. After you have written as much as you can, try asking those around you to help identify your strengths and weaknesses too. Be very aware of these things. After all, awareness will bring success—and we are in this industry to be successful!

Overcoming Life's Obstacles

As much as I love our industry, there are so many myths and misconceptions about what we do. Some of the misconceptions people outside the industry have about us are that we harass our friends and family, annoyingly talk to everyone, don't truly understand business, and don't have a legitimate career. On the contrary, people within the industry make it seem like all is perfect, that success will come over night, and with very little work you can make millions of dollars and be living on a yacht.

First off, this is not the case and I would honestly say it is quite the opposite. I see network marketers as a group of individuals with a career path that requires skill, dedication, and hard work. It's an industry that can offer flexibility, build character, and develop individuals into something more. I see the industry as one that can produce substantial returns and positively impact the lives of others in many ways. However, it doesn't mean it comes easy or without obstacles.

Truthfully, life can just suck at times and there is not much we can do about it. I can think of many times in my life that I was getting so close to good things happening and then something would come up—and it usually was not something enjoyable. I'm sure you can relate to this to some degree. There is nothing more frustrating, annoying, and irritating than these obstacles slowing us down and getting in the way of our success. However, we don't have to focus on the obstacles themselves, just on ways to overcome them.

Let me suggest a few ideas that I use to overcome obstacles in my life and in my business:

- **Anticipate Obstacles** - No matter how great life may seem or how good you are at business, it is important to anticipate that obstacles will arise. This anticipation can help you prevent your goals from being completely hijacked. Yes, sometimes obstacles can slow down progression, but it's better to progress slowly than to come to a complete stop. Roll with the punches as best you can, but stay focused and move forward.

- **Stay Positive** - As hard as it may be at times, remember to be optimistic and positive. Sometimes your efforts to stay positive will be all that keeps you moving forward, but I strongly believe that this practice has true power to make your dreams happen.

Tip: Show your team that you are positive and excited. This does not mean you can't be real with them, but helping them see that you are a positive person is something they will end up duplicating with their teams. Everything we do in the industry needs to be able to be duplicated and this starts with our positive attitude.

- **Focus on Your "Why"** - Focusing on your "why" will keep you positive, motivated, and focused on the bigger picture. By keeping your ultimate goal in mind, obstacles can easily be put into perspective and seen as only a minor delay in your quest to reach the summit.

- **Prepare an Emergency Plan** - Have a basic emergency plan ready to be used when obstacles hit. By having this plan it makes the obstacle much more tolerable and able to be conquered. Keep this plan in your back pocket at all times and be prepared for anything.

- **Find a Venting Partner** - It's true, we all need someone to vent to at times. So find someone that will listen to you, hear you out, and at the end of the chat will kindly and directly encourage you to keep moving forward. Venting is beneficial. Constant negativity and wallowing in misery is destructive. So do what you need to and then get back to work.

Tip: When selecting a venting partner, be careful who you vent to. It's important that we don't complain to our downlines even if they are our friends or family. Be real, open, and honest with them, but don't have a full-on venting session. You need to be seen as a positive leader and someone they can go to for support and guidance. Push your complaints upward or outward to your upline and never to your downline.

I realize that I've spoken about obstacles in a general way. Each of us have our own obstacles, challenges, and mountains to climb. These obstacles can be related to our personal lives, someone close to us, or our business. I have found when times get tough it helps to identify the problem, provide solutions, and come up with resources to help conquer the problem. Try the following activity when times get tough or if you can't seem to find a solution for the obstacles you're currently facing. Simply list out your problem(s) in one column, then write out some possible solutions in the next column, and finally, list out possible resources you can think of that can assist you in your solutions. See the following table for an example:

Identify the problem	Possible solutions	Resources to assist
Decline in volume	• Work with team • Set prospecting goals • Hold additional classes	• Use strengths of team members • Talk with everyone • Prepare better for classes

Tip: Take time to identify the problem, expound in depth on the solutions, and identify resources available to you. Repeat this exercise as often as needed to help overcome your obstacles.

Don't Give Up

I am going to be super real with you for a few moments and tell it like it is. If you're going to succeed in this business you've got to eliminate the idea of giving up. It simply can't be an option. Whether you're just starting out or have been in the industry for years, if you're contemplating the idea of giving up, this is not the industry for you. There are going to be days that it straight up sucks! Life is going to kick you down, your business builders are going to struggle, customers will stop purchasing, you won't find new prospects, and you will have doubts—but guess what? That is what you signed up for. Success isn't just built on a dream, but through adversity and hard work.

However, there is great news! You're working in an industry with limitless opportunities for you to succeed. It will bring you more success than you could ever imagine, but nothing comes easy. As you work hard and are persistent in your efforts, you will unlock the opportunities available to you. Like climbing to the summit of a mountain, you will have to take steps to get there. With the correct training, tools, guidance, and persistence you will reach your goal.

As you keep momentum moving forward, you will find that you will get stronger, work smarter, and operate faster. Think about the first time you learned how to ride a bike. You might have started with training wheels, then attempted to ride with the help of someone stabilizing you, and eventually you were able to ride on your own. Most of us likely fell over or crashed once or twice, but you eventually learned how to master the skill of bike riding. Just like the bike analogy, each situation you go through with your business will provide valuable lessons and experiences that you can apply to new situations. You might not be perfect at first, but you will get to a point where you are able to help others overcome the same obstacles.

Tip: Start an obstacle journal. Every time something comes up or gets in your way, write about it. This is a great way to be real with yourself, open up, and to have something to remind you of the hard times and lessons learned from them. Keep this journal in a place where you can always find it and come back to it. Your team will be able to learn greatly from the obstacles you have faced and the way you have overcome them.

Going through obstacles can help develop you into not only a better person, but also into an empathetic leader. Some of the best leaders in my life were the ones who took the time to connect with me and relate their experiences to my situation. Like you, I can think of many times I questioned if I could succeed or be the leader that my team needed me to be. If I could have seen what the future held for me, the success I was destined to have, and the difference I could make with others, it would have changed my entire perspective. If I was able to make this happen, so can you.

I am now able to relate my experiences to those I work with in ways I would have never been able to. We may never really understand why things happen or go the way they do, but I know that through our experiences we are shaped into the person we need to be—and by being the best version of you, your business will succeed. Keep working hard and don't give up. Success is just around the corner.

Avoiding Burnout

Have you ever been so numb to doing something you simply did not care what happened when you were done? This, my friend, is a sign of burnout—and it sucks! But before you beat yourself up over feeling this way, you have to realize that this is normal for a lot of individuals. It's true that success takes a lot of hard work, but we all have limits. If you have reached this point in your business or life, let me suggest a few ideas to help you progress past the current feeling of burnout and how to avoid it in the future:

- **Take a Timeout** - If you are feeling overwhelmed and burned out, stop. Take a timeout for yourself. Stop working, turn off your phone, and simply take a moment to reset. Go for a walk, meditate, exercise, or do something you enjoy doing. Investing in yourself will help you become more effective in your life and in your business. It's important to focus on *you* for a period of time. After all, people are not only buying your product or service, they're purchasing because of you! So take some time to relax, refresh, and regroup.

- **Evaluate Your Circumstance** - When I've reached a moment of burnout, I like to take some time to evaluate the circumstances that lead up to it. I suggest you do the same. This will help you understand the reasons that caused your burnout and increase your awareness of those triggers in the future.

- **Set Goals** - After you have rested and now feel like you can get back to it, I want you to take a few minutes to set some goals. What are you going to do to avoid this in the future? What are you going to do to succeed? How will you be more passionate and more focused than before? You can even give yourself a little pep talk.

• **Get Back to Work** - Now that you're refreshed and excited about your new goals, get back to work. It's important to give yourself enough time to reset, but be sure to resume the work. Don't delay, keep the momentum moving forward, stay focused, and you will see results.

Burnout is a normal part of life and it is something we must address and fix. Avoid it as much as possible, but when it happens—because it will happen at least once—focus on the steps listed above and don't give up. Make the time to focus on becoming the best version of you, your personal development, and making your goals and dreams a reality.

To Do List

- [ ] Define your "why"

- [ ] Identify three ways you can start living your "why" today

- [ ] Create a list of your top five strengths and weaknesses

- [ ] Select two of your business builders and have them identify five of their strengths and weaknesses

- [ ] Create an emergency plan to help overcome obstacles

- [ ] Start an obstacle journal

- [ ] If you're feeling burned out, take a break and refresh

Tip: To learn more, follow me at facebook.com/trainwithjustin

Chapter Notes

Chapter 2
Marketing

Marketing is one area that I have come to realize most people simply don't understand, nor do they really grasp the importance of what good marketing is and how it can really make a difference in their business. Over the years, I have heard many people say things like, "I don't need to do marketing, my company does that for me," or "Why would I need a brand or a marketing plan?" One of the things that sets successful individuals apart from those who are not successful, is the fact that they truly understand and implement marketing into their business efforts without counting on others to do that part of the business for them.

The definition of marketing is simply the act of promoting and selling a product or service, which could include advertising, analytics, content, promotions, and so on. Having a complete and effective marketing plan and strategy will effectively incorporate these different tactics to increase the exposure of your business. This can help accelerate the growth of your business in a big way. Marketing can be both scientific and creative. There are tactics that will help you be successful by following a formula (do x or y and you'll accomplish z), and others that will require you to be creative and think outside of the box. Typically the latter will require some experimentation about what works and what doesn't work in your unique situations and efforts. However, both will contribute to your overall success in your business.

Creating Your Personal Brand

One of the great things about this industry is that we work with companies that likely already have a developed and established brand, a solid product or service, and a unique niche market. Like these companies, you also need to have a personal brand, a way to set yourself apart from others. Branding can simply be defined as the way others perceive you in their interactions with you or your business. These interactions could be in person, over the Internet, in writing, over the phone, through advertisements, or a number of other ways. When I mention branding and the importance of having a personal brand, most people don't understand what I mean, nor do they understand the importance of having their own personal brand. Have you ever thought about what makes you different or unique from the others within your company? What makes someone want to work with *you*

26

instead of another representative from your company? The answer to this is *your brand.*

There are several ways to set yourself apart from others in the industry, but before we get into all of the ways to do that in your business, I want you to think about other companies that you interact with or admire. What makes them stand out in your mind? For most of them it's probably a recognizable logo, the customer service they provide, the quality products they sell, or the causes they represent. I want you to think about these other companies to realize what goes into creating a brand and then I want you to think about how it relates to you and your business.

How do your customers feel about you? How do you interact with them? How do they feel when they work with you? Do you have a logo? If so, what colors do you use? Is it memorable? Is it easily recognizable? What are the products or services you offer? Why do you enjoy them? What do they say about you? Do you represent a cause? If so, why do you care about it? I really want you to start thinking about these things because you will want to stand out somehow. I'm not necessarily saying you need to have all of these things, but with a little effort and consistency your customers and business builders will come to expect a specific experience from you—and this will help you stand out.

Aside from what I just discussed, here are several others ways that your brand can be reflected to your customers and business builders:

- **Social Media** - What is the name of your page or group? Do you use bright pictures? Do you have consistent and recognizable content? Do your groups and pages have a consistent appearance?

- **Writing** - What is the voice you write in? Is it playful? Serious? Factual? Do you write a blog? Think about your approach whenever you write. Obviously, there are different circumstances that you might write in, but by being consistent it will help others recognize you and your brand.

- **Interactions** - Do you leave thank you cards? Do you give small gifts to your business builders? Do you share motivational quotes? Hold classes? Provide surveys? Host a podcast or a video channel?

This is a simple list of ideas—it is not an all encompassing list, nor is it something that you have to determine down to the exact detail. A brand does not need to be created before you start building your business. Brands constantly change and evolve over time. As you revise your quarterly marketing plan, you can make updates and adjustments to your brand.

Remember that we are in an industry that depends on making and maintaining great relationships. Creating a personal brand will help others easily recognize your business and build quality relationships between you, your customers, and business builders.

> **Tip:** It can sometimes be overwhelming when you start to create your personal brand. Start small and use the steps below to get started:
> - Select two or three colors. Consistently use these when you create materials (e.g., fliers, graphics, etc.).
> - Think about and create a fun logo that is specific to you and your business.
> - Select two or three fonts and use them consistently in your materials (e.g., newsletters, graphics, etc.)
> - Create a level of excellence for your customers and stick to it (i.e., customer service standards).

Marketing Plan: 6 Steps

As mentioned previously, marketing can have a big impact on the growth of your business and how quickly it grows. However, in order to see the best results, you'll need to have a plan to implement your efforts in the right way—so let's dive right into creating a solid marketing plan. Trying to market without a plan is like shooting an arrow at a target without aiming. Marketing plans give you the aim you need to hit the bullseye.

Step 1: Perform a Situational Analysis

This is one of the most important steps in your plan—it's a time to be open, honest, and real with yourself to identify what's going on in your business. In this step we are going to identify everything—the good, the bad, and the ugly. Every other step depends on this one, so be open and make sure you identify exactly what's going on in your business.

Rate yourself on a scale from 1-10, with one being the lowest and ten being the highest. You'll find a list below to help you get started. Make sure to add in all other areas of your business and remember to be honest with how you rate your business.

1. **Education** - How well are you educating your business builders? Do your customers know enough about the products or services offered? Do they understand how your company works? Are you sufficiently educating your team?

 Reference: Please see the Education chapter in this book for more information on ways to successfully educate your team.

2. **Commissions** - Are you making the money you want to be making? Have you earned a check? Are your business builders earning money? Are you helping them earn the money they want to be making?

3. **Classes** - Are you teaching, presenting, and making yourself heard? Are you good at teaching? Are your classes clear?

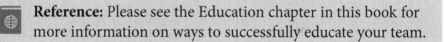 **Reference:** Please see the Classes chapter in this book for more information on hosting successful classes.

4. **Leadership** - Do you see yourself as a leader? Are you helping your business builders become leaders? Does your team look to you and see you as a leader?

> **Reference:** Please see the Leadership chapter in this book for more information on becoming the best leader and developing others to become leaders.

5. **Monthly Volume** - Is your volume consistently growing? Are you stagnant? How far away are you from your goal?

6. **Prospecting** - Are you finding new prospects? Are you enrolling new customers and business builders monthly? Is your team actively growing?

> **Reference:** Please see the Prospecting chapter in this book for creative ways to find new people and to start the 60-day Prospecting Plan.

7. **Social Media** - Are you using social media? Do you have a following that is consistently growing? Do you utilize pages and groups on Facebook? Do you have sufficient interaction?

8. **Team Participation** - Is your team excited? Do they participate in what you're doing? Do they go silent when you ask them to do something? Do you feel like you're the only one working and seem to get frustrated with your team?

Grading Rubric

1-3 If you graded yourself in this range then this is a clear indication that your business could use more development in this specific area. Don't beat yourself up, this is a great starting point.

4-7 If you graded yourself in this range then it means that your business is on the right path, but has some room for improvement. Keep giving some love to these areas and stay focused on constantly improving.

8-10 If you graded yourself in this range then you are well on your way to becoming an excellent marketer! Continue to develop these areas when and where you can.

Again, these items are just a few examples of different things going on in your business and there could and should be more. By evaluating yourself and seeing really where you stand it becomes super simple to see what areas you are doing well in and what areas need improvement. Make sure to pick areas very specific to your business.

Step 2: Identify Your Demographic

Who is your target audience or the group of people you're wanting to reach? And not only that, but who are the individuals that would benefit most from your products or services? Have you thought about this before? And whatever you say, please don't think you're targeting everyone. It is important to focus on more specific individuals or groups so your efforts and message can be more precise and effective. Consider a toy store, would they market to people who don't have kids? Or people who don't play with toys? They focus in on those who are going to understand their product and want to purchase it. The more you can understand your target audience the better you can reach them in your marketing efforts. By doing this you are saving time, energy, and money by being smarter.

You could spend a lot of time, money, and energy trying to market to everyone and never be successful. Focusing on your demographic allows you to hone in on who it is you want to be working with and how you can help them— but more particularly, people who actually want to use your company's products or services.

> **Tip:** Keep in mind your personal demographic may change. You many move to a new neighborhood, city, state or even country. Focus on selecting a type of person, an age group, or other specific groupings like these, so if your life circumstances change then you don't have to start over with your efforts. However, it's ok for your demographic to change from time to time. As we progress in life at times our circle of friends might change, our connections might be different, or we might develop new interests and hobbies— all of which would put us in contact with different people. You should be able to connect with your demographic, but keep in mind it should also stretch you to come out of your comfort zone.

Take some time to get to know your demographic. Who are these individuals? What do they like? What don't they like? What are their hobbies? What are their buying trends? How can you help them? What do you bring to the table that grabs their attention or benefits them? Do your best to narrow it down. Sometimes you'll have to give it your best educated guess, so it's important to work with individuals and be aware of their personalities, likes, dislikes, etc.—and take note. You can always come back to this step to add, delete, or update the information as you get to know your demographic better. Look at the example below to give you an idea about how to get started:

Individual or Group	Detailed Description of Individual or Group	How Can You Help Them?
Working Moms (Age 20-35)	• They are driven • They want to provide a good living environment for their children and family • They don't have a lot of time for extracurricular activities • They enjoy current fashion trends • They use Instagram and Facebook in their moments of free time to keep up with their family and friends • They surf Pinterest before they go to sleep to wind down	• Teach them plans to work smarter, not harder • Company knowledge • Have several working moms on the team • Show them ways your products or services can save them time and make their lives easier • Have an understanding of social media and help them to use their following to grow a business

Again, this is just an example to help get you started. Take time to identify your demographic and really break down who they are and how you can help them. This will help you in your efforts to connect with and reach them.

Step 3: Set Realistic Goals

I am a huge fan of setting goals and truly believe they can have a huge impact on your business. However, goals can also be a stressor if they are not set correctly. When setting goals they need to be relevant to your business, measured by time, and achievable. Make sure they will challenge and stretch you to make things happen, but also be realistic to accomplish.

During this step you're going to set goals for yourself and for your team. You need to use the information from Step 1 of the Marketing Plan, to help guide you in creating appropriate goals to grow your business, fix your current situation, and keep momentum moving forward. Remember, it is important to be detailed with your goals. Include all details within the goal such as a date to accomplish it by, who you will need to work with, and so on. A detailed goal is a money-making goal.

Step 4: Develop Strategies

Now that we have made it to Step 4, it is time to really get things going and put your goals into action to improve your current situation. Each and every goal should have a set strategy or tactic to make the goal a reality.

Be sure to dive into the details when writing these out. What exactly do you need to do to make things happen? Who will be involved? What will it take to execute on these? See the example listed below for how your Marketing Plan should look up to Step 4:

Perform a Situational Analysis: Not finding people. Currently only finding maybe one person per month.

Identify Your Demographic: Working with both working and stay-at-home moms.

Set Realistic Goals: Sign up ten new people per month.

Develop Strategies:

1. Teach one class per week. Focus topics around things moms might be interested in. Start classes by a set date.

2. Follow the 60-day Prospecting Plan to talk with new people daily.

3. Invite two people per day to weekly classes.

4. Use Tom, Maria, and Christina (business builders) to help invite people to the classes. Christina works at a daycare and has contact with moms on a daily basis—help her find ways to talk with them. Maria stays at home and goes to a weekly mom's

group—help her come up with a creative way to talk about the company. Tom's mother is actively involved in the community—find ways to talk with her and get into her network of friends.

Be sure to complete the above activity for each of your goals. Take the time to be detailed and set specific plans to make each goal a reality.

Step 5: Create a Budget

Most people often forget about creating a budget for their marketing efforts, but it is something that is needed. It's important to remember at times you need to spend money to make money. However, you need to be smart about what you spend your money on. There are so many different resources available to help grow your business and it's important to select the ones that are going to have the biggest impact for the amount you spend.

As you start, I suggest not spending more than you make. There will be certain things that come up that might be an exception to this, however, generally this is something you should stick to. As your commission check goes up, your marketing budget should also increase to continue growing your business (sometimes you don't have the option to spend anything because you might need the money for something else—and that is ok). There are so many ways you can grow your business without spending a penny. Just be sure to update the budget as you start making more money.

Step 6: Implement Action Items

This section is simple and yet vital to the success of your Marketing Plan. Now that you have set goals and listed strategies and tactics to make those goals happen, it's time to put them into action. Don't fall into the trap of being someone who plans and plans, but never actually gets anything done. A perfect plan without action is an unsuccessful plan. Set small steps to make things happen. See the example below about how your Marketing Plan should look after completing all six steps:

Perform a Situational Analysis: Not finding people. Currently only finding maybe one person per month.

Identify Your Demographic: Working with both working and stay-at-home moms.

Set Realistic Goals: Sign up ten new people per month.

Develop Strategies:

1. Teach one class per week. Focus topics around things moms might be interested in. Start classes by this day.

2. Follow the 60-day Prospecting Plan to talk with new people daily.

3. Invite two people per day to weekly classes.

4. Use Tom, Maria, and Christina (business builders) to help invite people to the classes. Christina works at a daycare and has contact with moms on a daily basis—help her find ways to talk with them. Maria stays at home and goes to a weekly mom's group—help her come up with a creative way to talk about the company. Tom's mother is actively involved in the community, find ways to talk with her and get into her network of friends.

> **Tip:** Remember to include your budget here, when you have strategies or tactics that have an associated cost to them.

Implement Action Items:

1. Take ten minutes per day and create content for weekly classes.

2. Complete daily activities on 60-day Prospecting Plan by noon.

3. Work with Maria to start inviting people from her mom's group.

Again, the goal of this step is to simply get you moving forward and implementing your Marketing Plan. Be more detailed here and really set small steps to accomplish your bigger goals.

> **Tip:** You can't be detailed enough in Step 6 of the Marketing Plan. If you're able to break it down into monthly, weekly, or even daily goals this will ensure you accomplish your overall goals.

Now that you have created a Marketing Plan, make sure to come back at least every three months and revise your plan. Look at the things you have accomplished over that period of time and set new goals, update the plan, and keep working. Things constantly change and it's important your plan changes to match that. However, don't change your plan if something has not happened or if you did not get to something because you did not feel like it. Simply keep updating and make it work.

Promotions and Incentives

Promotions are defined as something that raises awareness of a product or brand, generates sales, creates brand loyalty, and encourages individuals to learn more about or be more involved with your cause. Incentives are defined as using prizes and rewards to encourage business builders to grow their business.

Most companies typically offer regular promotions and incentives and it's important to know and understand the details about these, and to share them with your customers and business builders. Learn the details of these—how long they're offered, what products or services are included, or if any restrictions or limitations apply. Knowing the details about the promotions and incentives will help you know how to promote them effectively. Oftentimes company promotions will occur on a consistent basis, which makes it easy for you to plan for. Capitalize on these as best you can because they can be a great motivation for both your customers and business builders.

Along with the promotions and incentives that your company offers, it also helps to offer your own promotions and incentives for your customers and business builders. It could be something to give them an extra push of motivation and something that will set you apart from others. When creating your promotions and incentives, it's important to keep in mind that the goal is to provide value and to help your customers and business builders experience success. Promotions can be used to offer discounts, free items, and chances to win giveaways. They create excitement for your customers while educating them on your company's products or services. Incentives act the same as promotions, but for your business builders.

The great thing about marketing with promotions and incentives is it allows you to be creative—and there is no wrong type of promotion or incentive. Simply do your best and offer something that will add value and motivate. You will find a list below of some of the most common types of promotions and incentives. Again, remember these can be done on any budget and work for anyone of you at any phase in your business.

Types of Promotions:

- **Discounted Items** - Discounted promotions are quite popular and really can help motivate your customers. Oftentimes companies will do this as a promotion—and it's something you can do too. These are designed to boost, add value to, and encourage purchases of new and existing products or services. Be smart when discounting these items because the goal is to help grow your business, not to lose money on the promotion—so don't go overboard. Usually for this type of promotion, I would discount the items no more than 10-15%.

- **BOGO** - Buy one, get one is another highly used promotion and it's one that really gets customers excited and moving forward. People love getting things for free, and if that means they have to purchase something to get something for free, oftentimes they will do it. Again, be smart with this and don't give everything away. Make sure they are purchasing something with a higher value than the item you're giving away.

- **Free Shipping** - This is quite an easy promotion to offer and again, using the word "free" really motivates people. Simply reimburse them for the shipping on orders placed within a certain time frame. When doing this you can set specific qualifications so you're only paying shipping on set items—a certain weight or at a set dollar amount.

- **More** - This has become one of my favorite promotion types and can really help boost your volume and encourage people to purchase more. This promotion focuses on existing customers that order on a regular basis and is just what it says it is. You encourage these customers to spend a bit more, maybe an extra 5, 10, or 20 dollars—something more than they normally order. Take your customers who order monthly and encourage them to add just a bit more to their order and if they do they will qualify for something special. I usually enter these people into a drawing. They get one entry per every extra amount they spend over their normal order value and a set amount of winners will be selected to win a certain gift.

- **Share What You Love** - Even though your customers may not be interested in doing the business, it never hurts to give them a reason to share something they love. Encourage them to share something they love about the company, make a post on Facebook, talk with a friend, etc. For each person they share with, they will get an entry into a drawing and a select amount of individuals will receive a gift.

> **Tip:** Remember not to push your customers to do the business. However, never cross them off as a potential business builder. Oftentimes they will become your best builders, but it simply happens in their own time. Be there to support them, give them opportunities from time to time to promote your company, and be ready when they decide to grow a business.

- **Frequent Flyer** - Reward your frequent customers. Give them reasons to purchase on a regular basis and thank them for doing so. Oftentimes I will do this in three month periods. For example, if they purchase a set amount of product for three months, they will get a predetermined gift, then again at six months, nine months, and so on. The entire goal of this is to keep them purchasing and give them reasons to do it on a regular, consecutive basis.

> **Tip:** Take time to decide on your gifts before promoting them to your customers. This allows you to budget correctly to get them gifts they will be excited to receive.

Types of Incentives

- **Enrollment** - Simply offer a prize, an entry for a drawing, or something else for individuals who enroll a certain amount of people in a set period of time. This is a great way to excite your business builders and get them talking to people.

- **The Most** - Be creative here and simply incentivize those that do the most of something. For instance, you could offer an incentive for the person who teaches the most classes, or for the biggest increase in volume, or something similar. Give them something small that motivates them and helps get them excited about being their best and stretching themselves to do a bit more.

- **Retreat Trips or Getaways** - These are typically bigger incentives for your business builders, but can be quite fun. Typically these larger incentives would take place over a period of several months and should help you see quite a large increase in your business and paycheck. It's important to strategically plan these out and make sure you can cover the trip in your budget. They can really motivate your business builders to make things happen.

Tip: Be sure to stretch your business builders to grow their business while striving to receive the incentives. However, make sure it is something that is achievable and will motivate them instead of discourage them.

Again, these are just a few ideas of common promotions and incentives, but they really do work and make a difference with your business. Think about ways you can implement some type of promotion or incentive in your business today. Before creating and implementing your promotions and incentives, it's important to understand what needs to be considered when successfully creating these.

First and foremost, think about if your promotion or incentive will give you a return on investment (ROI). Not all promotions and incentives will make their money back, and that's ok. An ROI could come back in many ways; it could be that you have excited customers, more customers purchasing, business builders stepping up to work and grow their team, and so on. But at the end of the day, whatever way it happens, you need to have some sort of return and make sure your promotion or incentive is improving your business.

When considering a promotion or incentive it's important to keep the timing in mind. Are you giving yourself enough time to plan it, promote it, and execute it successfully? In order for these to be a success, timing really is everything—and not only for you, but your customers and business builders too. Are you giving them enough time to act, be motivated, and to make things happen without giving them too much time where they might procrastinate or lose interest in what you're doing? Promotions and incentives should add a sense of urgency to what you're doing and get people to act sooner rather than later. However, don't make them feel rushed or pressured.

In addition to considering the correct timing for a promotion or incentive, it's also important to consider what the reward will be. This may be a discount, a trip, an entry in a drawing, or something simple, but it needs to be enough to motivate and encourage your team to work towards whatever the promotion is trying to accomplish. If you're trying to get customers to purchase something extra with a promotion, it needs to be something that they can't already find somewhere else for less and it needs to be something that will add value to their life—enough to motivate them to go the extra mile. If you're working to motivate your business builders with an incentive, it's important to make sure the reward outweighs the work they may have to do to accomplish it.

Finally, you need to think about the end goal or outcome when considering a promotion or incentive and what you need to do to make it successful. How do you want your customers to feel after a promotion? How excited do you want your business builders to be at the end of an incentive? You want to stretch them, take them outside of their comfort zones, and help them to feel accomplished at the end. Oftentimes this step is forgotten and is something that really needs to happen to help guarantee the success of a promotion.

Tip: Oftentimes when creating promotions, it helps to start with the end goal and work your way back to the beginning of the promotion. Decide what it is you want to accomplish. This could be to promote new signups, encourage customers to purchase extra items, or something similar. Really know what it is you want the result to be. Once you have the end goal in mind, create the requirements and decide what will be given to motivate.

Tracking and Planning

One of the best ways to keep track of your promotions and incentives is by having them scheduled on a calendar. This will allow you to write down the details associated with your promotions and incentives, stay on schedule to promote and market them, and to contribute to the overall success of what you're doing. Oftentimes promotions and incentives are put together last minute and we later wonder why they were not successful. It's simply because it takes time to execute, market, and prepare these successfully.

It's important to plan your promotions and incentives about a month in advance, so by the second week of the month you're working on next month's calendar. Take time to really think your promotions out to make sure they make sense for your business and give yourself enough time to execute them successfully.

Tip: When tracking and planning your promotions, remember the holidays. Every holiday is an excuse for an exciting promotion, but you should start promoting it prior to the actual holiday. This will give others time to think about it and not take them away from their family or friends on the actual holiday.

In a typical month I would suggest doing no more than three promotions and one incentive. I am not meaning a number of items, but a number of actual promotion types. For example, you could have three products in one of your BOGO promotions, but this would still count as one promotion and not three. You want to be sure to not overwhelm your customers or business builders with too many promotions or incentives.

Also, you don't want them to create the mindset of only purchasing when you're offering something extra or special. Promotions and incentives are simply extras and help to grow a successful business. You never want them to expect you to do something.

> **Tip:** When thinking about promotions, remember people like options. Give them different options at different price points. Be careful not to give too many options and keep it simple, but give them the ability to choose what works best for them.

When launching your monthly promotions or incentives it's important to follow the 7-day Plan below to guarantee success:

- **Day 1** - *Share Promotions and Incentives* - Announce the promotion and incentive (This could be your company's promotions or incentives or a promotion or incentive you are offering for your team).

- **Days 2-4** - *Educational Promotion and Incentive Calls* - This is an opportunity to connect with three to five of your customers or business builders each day. Talk with them, connect with them, and share the promotions and incentives with them. Make sure they know how to take advantage of them and how to enjoy their benefits.

- **Day 5** - *Space and Time* - Oftentimes we want to encourage people to purchase or take advantage of a promotion or incentive, but we forget to give them time to actually think on it. Simply give them some space, but be there to answer questions if they have any—and be sure to take a break from actively promoting it.

- **Day 6** - *Promotion or Incentive Questions* - This is a more casual day, but basically let your customers and business builders know you're available to help them and answer their questions. You can do a post on one of your Facebook Groups or page, send a text message, or how ever you prefer to communicate with your team—but let them know you're there to answer questions for them.

- **Day 7** - *Promotion or Incentive Reminder* - Simply remind your customers and business builders about the promotions or incentives and the details including the time frame and steps that need to be taken in order to take advantage of it. Be there if they have questions.

Tip: Remember to create next month's promotion and incentive calendar by the 15th and 16th of the month.

Following the 7-day Plan will help guarantee your customers and business builders are informed about the new and exciting promotions and incentives. With promotions and incentives it's important to start out strong, but also to finish strong. Follow the steps below to help you in the final days of your promotion or incentive period:

- **Second to Last Day** - *Promotion or Incentive Hustle* - This is your chance to create urgency and get your customers and business builders excited and ready to act if they are planning on doing so during the period of time the promotion or incentive is offered. Remember to add value and help them see the benefit of this promotion.

- **Last Day** - *Final Reminder* - This is the last time to remind them to take advantage of the promotions or incentives during the period of time they are offered. Also take some time to get them excited about upcoming promotions and get ready to start over again.

Tip: If you're just getting started in your business, scale this plan down. Maybe you don't have the budget for multiple promotions, or you don't have business builders—and that's ok. Focus on what you do have and implement parts of this plan as you are able to. Eventually, you will be using the entire plan.

Social Media and Blogs

In the fast-paced world we live in, social media and Internet marketing is imperative to grow your business. Learning the basics, understanding how to use them for your business, and knowing the differences between platforms will make a huge difference to the success of your business. Social media can be quite overwhelming if you're just getting started, so start out small. Little by little you will "get it" and it will open the door to create an international business that will work for you 24 hours a day, 7 days a week. Social media has given me the opportunity to find, meet, and connect with people all over the world. When done correctly, it can have the same impact as meeting with them in person and having that personal connection we all need in business.

Facebook

Established: 2004
Monthly Active Users: Approximately 1.5 billion
Daily Active Users: Approximately 1 billion
Largest Age Demographic: 25+

Facebook is by far the most used social media platform and can be highly beneficial in building a business when used correctly. Oftentimes people misuse Facebook—they annoy their friends and they become the person that everyone dreads because everything they do is business focused. Facebook was designed to be a social platform, allowing people to connect, to stay in contact, and to be involved in each others' lives. So it's important to remember that your friends on Facebook are your friends for *you* and not necessarily your business. Sadly, our friends and family don't always share the same passion for our business as we do, and it can be hard to find the balance of what and when to share while not going overboard. With over 1.5 billion monthly users, you can't afford to not be on Facebook as a business owner.

Getting a following on Facebook can take time, but when you stay consistent, work at it, and have fun using it, you can grow a large following and see a huge increase in your sales, recognition, and so on. Follow these five "must dos" to be a Facebook success:

1. **Personal Profile** - Use your personal profile on occasion to promote your business. Like I said before, don't be one of those people who goes overboard and becomes crazy annoying—find the balance. Each of your posts needs to be something about you, something about your life, and something you enjoy doing. Naturally, your

business is a huge part of your life and can be posted about in this way. When you do post about your business, be sure to keep it a lighthearted post showing why you love your company, what it has done for you, and how it could help others. It should not be a sales post.

Oftentimes we get caught up with asking people to order or promoting the business while not giving the value that's needed to help someone make a decision. The key to success is adding value to your friends' lives and helping them to see the passion you have for your company through your posts. Typically, I would post no more than twice a week about your business and the other times about your life, or other fun and exciting things going on. Each of these posts needs to be accompanied with a fun image—something you have taken or something that you can relate with. Ultimately this is your profile and it needs to reflect you personally. Your friends need to see your natural personality and relate with you like they always have, not just to become a business prospect.

2. **Business Pages** - These pages are a great way to connect with people, find new prospects, and to teach about your business. Use this page to educate, teach about your product or service, and to help them see the benefits your company offers and why it's needed. Again, every post needs to have something to grab their attention and to motivate them.

> **Reference:** Please see the Education chapter in this book for more information on Facebook pages.

3. **Be Social** - After all, Facebook is a social media platform and it's designed to be social and to connect you with others. Get to know people and find common interests. The more people you connect with and get to know, the better it will help you grow your business. When connecting with people, legitimately look for people of interest and to build relationships with those people, not

just for another prospect. The goal of connecting is to add value to someone's life and to mutually benefit each other.

4. **Community and Yard Sale Pages** - These pages can be a great benefit to your business and are designed to sell items. The goal of using these pages is not to promote the business or to try to find business builders, but to build leads and connections. Oftentimes I will use these to post a few items from my company for sale to see what interest I receive back. I then work with these people and help them receive the item they are interested in. These groups can also be a great way of finding professionals in an area that you can work with.

Here's an example of a post I might do, "Looking for good realtors in the area!" Keep these posts simple and minimal, and when done correctly, they can help you generate a good amount of leads and potential business. Once you receive some references, be sure to contact these people to tell them they come highly recommended and that you want to talk to them about ways you can do business together. Again, the goal of social media is to connect—and this is a great way of doing that. Finally, like anything else on Facebook, you need to be smart and not go overboard on the amount of posts you do within a certain amount of time.

5. **Advertise and Boost** - Facebook offers the option to advertise and boost posts. Advertisements allow you to pay for ad space to promote a product or service. Boosts allow you to promote your posts for more exposure to a larger audience than you normally would be able to without it. Both of them give you the opportunity to target specific audiences. These can be great resources for your business when done correctly. It's important that you have consistent content on your business page before paying to advertise since these advertisements are connected with it and oftentimes lead people to view your page. Be strategic when spending money on advertisements. There are so many things you can do on Facebook for free and this should be the last thing to do once you have gotten comfortable with the steps listed above.

> **Tip:** When creating ads on Facebook you also have the option to promote them on Instagram. You'd likely select this option if you have an engaging picture accompanying the ad and are interested in receiving more exposure.

Instagram

Established: 2010
Monthly Active Users: Approximately 400 million
Daily Active Users: Approximately 200 million
Largest Age Demographic: 18-29

Instagram is by far the easiest platform to get a following on and to get people interested in what you have going on in your life. The great thing about Instagram is it's all designed around images. Take your phone with you and capture a nice picture, give it a brief description, and post it. It is simple and can be quite fun. This platform is not meant for long posts, sappy stories, or anything like that. One of the reasons people like it is there is so much less drama than other social media platforms. It makes people excited, inspired, or ambitious when they see your amazing pictures.

Just like Facebook, you need to be smart to not overdo it with the business posts. Remember, people are following you for you, and not always your business. Take pictures of your product or service in action and make occasional posts about what you do, but don't make this the bulk of your posts. Make it about your life and naturally your business will be a part of that. You never want to become that annoying friend that we all have on social media. Think before you post and have fun. Follow these five steps to help you become an Instagram success:

1. **Take Captivating Pictures** - Everything about Instagram is focused on your pictures. People see these and get excited wanting to see more about what you do—so make them good. Take pictures that show what your life is like, things you're passionate about, and so on. Really, just have fun with this and enjoy it.

> **Tip:** Keep in mind some pictures get more attention than others. For example, some popular types of pictures on Instagram include pictures of food, landscapes, fitness, and traveling.

2. **Interact** - Take interest in the images others post. Find things you like, ask questions, make comments, and be actively engaged and interested in what others post. This shows them that you care, but it also helps you be seen by others who will see your comments and potentially follow you. It's also a good idea to thank others when they comment on your posts. Tag them by name and say something like, "Thanks for the love!" or "I appreciate your kind words." You can also briefly ask them about something you saw on their page. This can open a brief dialogue and will motivate people to interact more with you.

3. **Keep It Short** - The image needs to be the main portion of your post. Keep the text short, lighthearted, and relevant. People access this platform from their mobile device, so it's important that they can see your picture and read what you have to say about it in a short amount of time.

4. **Use Hashtags** - Using hashtags will give more exposure to your posts because it will categorize your post and make it searchable by that term. As a general rule, I would include at least three to eight hashtags. Don't overwhelm people with a million hashtags. You want them to be relevant to your post too. For instance, if you were posting a picture of the outside of your home you might use the following hashtags: #homesweethome, #flowers, #weekend, #sunshine. The great thing about Instagram is that as you type in your hashtag it will immediately show you how many others have used that particular hashtag. So you'll want to use hashtags that have a large number of uses. Typically basic words or popular phrases will have higher uses like #flowers, #bucketlist, or #goals.

If you are in a specific location then use a hashtag that includes the location (e.g., #nyc, #timessquare, #statueofliberty, etc.); if you are posting about food then describe it (e.g., #yum, #lemonade, #foodie, #dessert, etc.); or if you are posting about your product or service, then use words associated with it (e.g., #favorite, #lifehack, #lifesaver, #cantlivewithoutit). Get creative and have fun with these.

> **Tip:** Hashtags are an amazing way to build your business using social media. However, don't go "hashtag crazy". It can be extremely annoying when someone uses hashtags for everything or creates a very long one! #wehaveallseenthatpersonthatturnseverythingintoahashtag

5. **Make it Public** - If you're trying to gain more followers, then you'll need to make your profile public. I know this could make some of you uncomfortable, but you just need to be smart about this. You want to post things about your life, but if you know it is going to be public, then you might choose to be more selective on what you post. Keep your posts professional and tasteful. One advantage of making your profile public is that your posts can have more reach. A word of caution—when you make your profile public, a host of people or organizations may start following you. You're welcome to add those individuals or organizations, but use common sense when selecting which ones to follow.

Twitter

Established: 2006
Monthly Active Users: Approximately 310 million
Daily Active Users: Approximately 500 million tweets
Largest Age Demographic: 18-49

Twitter is another amazing platform to use that will allow you to connect with people and organizations. It allows you to share posts about things going on in your life with a limited amount of characters.

It's crucial that you keep your posts short because of these limits and it's a great way to connect people back to your blog, website, etc. Use Twitter to connect with people and get them to see more about what you have to offer.

Twitter can take a bit more time to get a following than the other two platforms. However, once you have followers they are usually interested in what it is you have to say and pay more attention to your tweets. Apply these six tips to be successful using Twitter in your business:

1. **Smart Links** - Connect people with your blog using smart links (Links made shorter so they fit within the character limit given by Twitter). Tweet something fun that captures their attention, then expound on it using your blog.

2. **Use Hashtags** - Twitter, like Instagram, uses hashtags to categorize and keep up with trending topics. Use them appropriately to help grow your following. Keep in mind that Twitter limits your characters, so you'll need to be very selective and strategic with these.

3. **Exciting, Relevant, and Concise** - Tweets should be exciting and capture the reader's attention. You only have 140 characters to make it count, so keep it short, to the point, and make sure you really prioritize what you're going to say.

4. **Be Patient** - As mentioned before, Twitter can take some time to gain a following. Be consistent and continue to tweet. Make sure you're connecting them to quality content and over time you will see an increase of followers and interaction.

5. **Interact with Others** - Take time to read other's tweets. This is a great way to find common interests, find ways to work together, and to connect. Twitter, like other social media platforms, is a two-way street, it's important to not just post content, but to interact and show appreciation for things others tweet. Like, comment on, or share other's tweets.

6. **Follow Influencers and Relevant Individuals or Organizations-** Search for influencers and relevant individuals or organizations that would be complementary to your industry or cause and follow them. Tag them from time to time in your tweets and try to interact with them. Make sure to be professional and respectful in your interactions. If this is something new to you then you might even find it fun.

> **Tip:** Have fun and tag business people, companies, celebrities and such when appropriate. This helps your post get seen and helps you connect with people. Others will see your tweet and potentially follow you.

> **Tip:** Have you ever said, "I have no interaction" or "I only get silence when I post"? Oftentimes this is because your content is not getting people engaged or excited. Are you really having a conversation with them or are you simply posting and hoping others engage?
>
> Think about this. If you were having a face-to-face conversation with someone, would you simply say, "Check out my product or service. It's great!"? This would never happen—or if it did, it would be awkward and not effective.
>
> Typically you would get them talking and interacting with you first and you should do the same on social media. If you ask clear questions and have clear expectations, you will start seeing more interaction.
>
> Also don't become "social media lazy"! So many people simply share a post or copy and paste something they saw and wonder why no one got involved. If you have seen the post, then most likely others have seen it too. Create your own content! Sharing other's content does have a place and time to be used, but this should not be the majority of your posts.

Blog

Blogging is a great way to share your story in more depth. It allows you to talk more about what you do and to let people into your life. In many ways, it can serve as an online journal, a place you can talk about your passions, fun things going on, and even your company. Oftentimes people will follow your blog and become interested in what you're saying based on the topic. Just like any of the other efforts discussed in this book, the goal of each blog post is to build value, to educate, and help others feel like they are not wasting their time by reading what you have to say. You'll find a list of tips and tricks below to help you get started building a blog and being successful at it:

1. **Have Fun and Be You** - Talk about what's going on in your life, what you enjoy doing, what your favorite passions might be, and so on. You want someone to be able to get to know you from what they read, and to really know what you're about and enjoy doing. If someone was to meet you after reading your blog they should be able to have a conversation with you like good friends would after a long time of not seeing each other. Talk about your business from time to time—but remember, the main goal of your blog is to allow people to connect with you.

2. **Share Your Blog Often on Social Media Platforms** - Reference your blog often using tweets on Twitter, pictures on Instagram, and posts on Facebook so people know about your blog and will follow you there as well. Include a link to your blog on business cards, email signatures and so on so people can get to know you.

Tip: Brand your blog. Make sure it really screams *you* and is consistent with your business brand. If your brand looks fun, your blog should look fun. If your brand is modern, your blog should be modern, and so on.

3. **Be Consistent or Don't Blog at All** - If you're going to have a blog, it's important that content is current and constantly being updated. If someone accesses your blog and can see it has been weeks or months since your last post, it is not going to look good and most likely they won't come back. Try to post something, even if it's small, twice a week. If you can only post once a week, that is ok as well, but no less than one time a week.

4. **Use Engaging Images, Show Videos, Etc.** - If you're teaching someone how to do something, don't just tell them, show them. Let them see pictures and videos—ones that really grab their attention and make them excited to do what you're doing. If you're blogging about your family, share pictures of your family; if you're talking about a vacation, show pictures from your vacation; if you're teaching someone to use your product or service, make a video.

5. **Connect with Other Relevant Bloggers** - Look for other bloggers that write about related topics associated with your industry and follow them. Read their blogs and interact with them when possible. This is a great way to expand your network and it might provide inspiration to you in your marketing efforts.

6. **Improve Over Time** - No one is going to be perfect at first, so don't wait for the perfect time to start. Sure, you want to plan out your content, but not to the point of waiting long periods of time. You can also read other blogs and look for ways that you feel they are successful. Then try to incorporate those into your efforts.

There are hundreds of ways to use the Internet and social media to grow your business—take advantage of these. We have just touched on a few ways you can start implementing these great resources. The key to everything you do online is being consistent. Notice I didn't say to be perfect. You will naturally get better over time, but it's also important to look for ways to improve. Keep in mind that you can't expect to have a large, interactive following if you only do it sporadically. Be consistent, stay focused, and start small. Have fun and you will see success.

To Do List

☐ Establish your brand

☐ Complete the 6 Steps of the Marketing Plan:

    ☐ Perform a situational analysis

    ☐ Identify your demographic

    ☐ Set realistic goals

    ☐ Develop strategies

    ☐ Create a budget

    ☐ Implement action items

☐ Schedule out your first month of promotions and incentives

☐ Pick three tips for social media and apply them

> **Tip:** To learn more, follow me at facebook.com/trainwithjustin

Chapter Notes

Chapter 3
Prospecting

What is Prospecting?

Prospecting is simply the act of being on the lookout and open to all possibilities of interacting with and meeting new people. We use a similar definition of prospecting within the industry. However, we take it one level deeper, understanding that not only are we constantly on the lookout, but we are prepared and ready to talk with anyone at any time, and we're constantly looking for new ways to find these people.

I remember when I started my first sales job and was responsible for prospecting a minimum of eight hours each day. After talking with over 30 prospects my first day, I was tired and discouraged because not a single person said "yes." The next morning I woke up and created a 60-day Prospecting Plan—similar to other plans I had created previously—and I was determined to use it and make it work. My plan had me talking to prospects daily and creating outlines that would help me develop the confidence to say the things I needed to be effective. Honestly, at first things did not get better. I was so frustrated and discouraged. I had an amazing plan to help guide me and I believed it would work, but I still had not closed a single sale nor had a single person show interest.

For some reason I was just not getting it, but as I reflected on what I was doing wrong it all started to make sense—the problem was me and my attitude. I was too impatient to wait for things to happen naturally, I was taking things too personally, and I was negative because people were not showing interest. The 60-day plan was just what I needed, but it came down to my approach. So I began to set goals to change my attitude. I became more open to talking with people and was determined that by having a better attitude and by following my 60-day plan, I would be successful.

Crazy enough, this attitude change happened quickly and I was surprised to hear my first "yes" the next day! Within the next five days I had over 20 people tell me "yes" and three people actually purchased from me. I was so excited! Surprisingly those numbers continued growing until one week I not only became the top seller in my area, but within the entire organization. The skills I learned through this experience and using the 60-day plan have changed my life, and continue to do so. If you're determined to make this happen, you can do it. All you need is a good attitude and the right plan. However, before you become a master prospector it's important to understand what prospecting is not and how to avoid these things.

> **Tip:** Take some time to evaluate your attitude. Are you positive? Or are you oftentimes negative? Do you focus on the negative aspects about your life and business? How do you feel about prospecting, marketing, your team, and other business matters? Be honest and open with yourself. Also ask someone close to you that knows you well to evaluate your attitude towards your business.

The Myth About Prospecting

Take a moment and briefly put yourself in the following scenario:

I have found a company that I like. I am excited and passionate about what they offer and about the money that I can make with them. Now it's time to talk with all my friends and family about it. If they say they are not interested, that is ok because I will keep talking with them, pushing them, and persuading them to join the company. If it is the correct thing for me, then it must be the correct thing for everyone else.

They may not see the success or the opportunity now—and they may think I am a bit crazy—but that's ok because I really know best and they don't know what they are missing out on. It is my duty to make sure they get involved one way or another. If they say no a second time, I will just invite them over and have a class set up. They won't know about it until they get here, but once they do, they will surely join because they will have seen how amazing it is.

Does this seem familiar? Maybe a little embellished? Sadly it's not too far off from situations that happen everyday within the industry.

It's time to open your eyes. How many of you have been this way before with friends and family? How many have done this without even thinking you're doing it? How many times have you heard others do this? How many times have you talked to someone who has had a bad experience with network marketers or their companies because someone has pushed them away?

I am going to be real with you for a few minutes. As a colleague in the industry, please stop being this person! You are not only hurting your business, but you're also hurting the rest of our businesses. By doing this you are giving a negative impression to prospects before they even get to speak with you or hear about your company. This is not prospecting, recruiting, networking, or anything similar to it. It is simply being annoying, harassing, and being someone that no one will want to work with. As we move through this section, I will explain ways you can be a successful business person while prospecting everyone, without being anything like these examples. If this is you, someone on your team, or someone you know, commit today to stop being this way. Together we can successfully prospect and change the image of our industry.

> **Tip:** Identify business builders who may come across as annoying, harassing, or as less than ideal. Sit down and help them to see a better way to grow their business. Be careful not to make them feel attacked. You want them to leave this conversation feeling motivated and uplifted with a clear plan to become better.

Over the next several sections we will be discussing things you need to know to become a master at prospecting. Once you master these techniques and follow the 60-day Prospecting Plan, you will be unstoppable and your business will soar.

Making a Connection

Before you start talking to prospects, it's important to have a few things established. Do you truly have a genuine connection with your company? Do you believe in the product or service, and know it is everything your company says it is? When times get tough and rumors spread, or prospects question what you're saying, do you still believe and support your company because you have experienced the difference it makes in your own life? Do you genuinely believe in your business opportunity and know you and others can make money and see success from it?

If you can't answer yes to at least one of these questions, this would be your first step. You should love the company you represent, be passionate about their products and services, and be confident that what you are doing makes a difference in others' lives and that you have something they can't live without. Simply having this belief and connection with your company will make you more confident, passionate, and much more successful in your efforts.

It's ok to have questions, doubts, or even concerns. Growing a genuine connection with your company can take time, and that's ok. But strive to use your product or service daily, study and learn about it, and work to make a personal connection with it. Once you do, you will notice a huge difference and those around you will also notice it too. After all, it's much harder for people to tell you no when you have a passion for and truly believe in something. Think about it. Have you ever listened to someone close to you talk about one of their favorite hobbies and because of their passion, you wanted to join in? Making a genuine connection with your product or service will help you to talk more naturally about it.

Tip: Take a few minutes to record two videos. In the first video, record yourself for two to three minutes talking about your business opportunity. Discuss what makes it a special opportunity, why you like it, and why others would benefit from it. In the second video, simply record yourself talking for two to three minutes about something you love or are passionate about outside of your business. This could be your family, a hobby, or anything that interests you. After you have made these videos, compare the two. Oftentimes we are much more passionate about our hobby or at least we are more comfortable talking about them and it shows. Channel some of that passion when talking about your business opportunity and you will begin to see more of a genuine connection to your company and its products or services.

Once you have at least one way to genuinely connect with your company, the next task is to connect with those you come in contact with. This is a step that is often forgotten when talking to prospects about your company. Do you take the time to get to know them? Do you help them get excited about what you're saying? Do you listen to what they have to say and understand where they are coming from? This is key! You must take the time to get to really know and connect with your prospects.

Now I am not saying you need to get to know their whole life story, but when you show interest in someone's life they will be open to trust you more. In turn, this will help open up more doors for you. Realize that some people have the ability to easily connect with others immediately after meeting them, while with others it takes more time. It doesn't matter which personality type you identify with, but your first goal should be getting to know your prospect and connecting with them. This comes way before presenting your company and telling them about a product or service you want them to buy.

Finding

One of the most difficult parts about prospecting is finding people to talk with. How many times have you told yourself, "I simply don't have anyone to talk to", "I can't get people to attend my classes", or "No one seems to be interested in what I have to say"? As I mentioned before, I have been there, I get it. Let's focus ourselves on finding new people and being committed to not giving up. With the techniques and ideas listed below, you will start to see a difference. Keep in mind that it doesn't happen overnight—it takes time—but the key is being consistent. As you follow the 60-day Prospecting Plan and set goals to find new people each day, this will pay off and you will soon look back and be in a very different situation.

The most common concern I hear is that people cannot find others to talk to about their company. They say their life doesn't allow them to come in contact with others, that they just don't have a big enough group of people to talk with, or a number of other concerns. I would go so far as to say this is the number one reason people leave the industry—they feel they don't have sufficient contacts to make their business successful. If you're saying this, do me a favor—stop! Commit to never getting caught up in saying this again. It simply brings negative energy into your business and it will slow your efforts down dramatically.

I understand that finding prospects can be hard, and at times it seems like you might not have anyone to talk to or work with. But guess what? That's part of the business and if you really take the time to evaluate your daily routine, you will see that there are tons of people you come in contact with on a regular basis. Oftentimes we blind ourselves to what we think a prospect is, or we give someone an option out before we even talk with them. How often do you say, "They won't be interested", "They are struggling and won't have the money", or "They don't believe in what we have to offer"?

When we do this we are presupposing people's situations or circumstances and we are likely missing out on those that would actually be interested and have the means to try what you have to offer. Always approach prospecting with an open mind, and never create an excuse for someone else. You may be surprised what results when you stop making excuses for others.

Next time you find yourself in this situation, evaluate your daily routine. Who do you see on a regular basis? Who do you talk with? Where do you go? Who are you around? This is key and I can promise you there are always ways to find prospects. This is an important concept to understand because it won't just be something you struggle with, but your team will also struggle with it at times. You will need to be able to help them recognize and evaluate the daily opportunities they have to contact others.

There are people out there that are ready to hear about your products or services today. Below you'll find a few examples of ways you could possibly come in contact with people. This does not include every possible way because we all have very different lives. However, pay close attention because this will help open your eyes to the endless possibilities you have with finding people.

- **Errands** - Do you ever get out of your house? Fill your car up with gas? Go to the store to buy items for your house or family? Do you take the kids to school? Go to the doctor? Pick something up for a friend? Take a book back to the library? These are just a few things that most people will have to do at some point in their life and they're great places to connect with others. How many times could you have talked with someone while running errands, but you chose not to? If you are honest with yourself you will be surprised by how many prospects you have missed. Don't miss out on these opportunities to talk with others and remember to connect with them in a genuine way. Don't just walk up to a stranger in the store and say, "Hey! I'm selling this. Do you want to buy one from me?" Keep it natural and connect with them.

- **Leisure Outings** - Do you ever take a break and get out? Do you go out to eat? Go to the movies? Take the kids to sports practice or games? Go shopping? Attend cultural or community events? If you don't do any of these, it's time to make a few changes and have some fun in your life. However, it's likely most of us do some of these activities from time to time. If you are enjoying an outing and not being open to finding prospects by talking to others then you're missing out on opportunities. I'm not saying you have to constantly be working, or that you can't take a break—sometimes it's needed to just not talk to anyone or think about business—but as a whole, I am confident you could do a bit more than what you're doing and that you would start seeing better results.

- **Employment** - Maybe this is not your main job at the moment, but guess what?!? That gives you an amazing opportunity to talk with people you work with and share what you do. Take time to build relationships and get to know these people. Be there to answer the questions they may have about your company and talk with them about your passions and life. Your business can be a passion and something you can share with colleagues when times are appropriate.

- **Neighborhood** - Do you live around other people? Do you have neighbors? Do you have an HOA? Do you talk with people in your neighborhood? Get to know these people—and where you already live in the same neighborhood, you should have many opportunities to connect on that level. Talk about the crazy neighbor (we all have one), something going on in the neighborhood, or just simply get to know them. As you do this you will have the opportunity to talk about your business.

- **Religious and Self Improvement Activities** - Do you attend church? Do you attend a support group? Do you attend meetings to better yourself? Again, this a great way to connect with people and get to know them. Genuinely connect with them, and when the time is right you will be able to talk about your business.

- **Fitness** - Do you work out? Do you attend aerobic, yoga, or weight training classes? Swim at a community pool? Participate in local races or other active groups? This is another opportunity to connect with people over something you have in common. Talk about fitness, talk about your goals, and get to know these people. Again, as you do this, you will at some point have the opportunity to talk with them about your business.

> **Tip:** Create a list of ideas of places, interactions, or ways to meet people—and keep it with you at all times. When you're not sure how to find people, reference this list. Constantly be adding new ideas to the list.

As previously stated, these are just a few examples to get you thinking about places and opportunities you come in contact with others—but seriously though, the options are limitless! Every time you find yourself saying you have no one to talk with, simply evaluate your daily routine and think about all of the regular interactions you have with people. Stop missing these opportunities because your business success depends upon it!

Once you have evaluated your current routines and are working those correctly, it's time to step out of your daily routine and put yourself in places to meet new prospects. Stepping out of our routine may seem a bit daunting or complicated at first, but it can be simple. Instead of working at home go to a coffee shop, sit at the library, or take an Uber to the store—simply get out of your house and put yourself in a new place. As you do this, you will not only come into contact with new people, but you will start building relationships. Finding prospects does not have to be as hard as we make it out to be, but a simple change to your routine could be the change needed to make all the difference in the world.

Luckily for all of us, we live in a world where the Internet makes it super easy to connect with others and to find new prospects. Social media, when used correctly, can be a great way to meet new prospects, change up your regular routine, and help you grow a successful business. Use the Internet and other technology to your advantage. Get to know people, but just keep in mind, it's important to connect with them.

When it comes down to it, the goal is simply to get noticed and be seen. This can be done in many ways, and honestly, can be quite simple. We oftentimes complicate it more than it needs to be. When you're out and about, use your product or service to help others see it in action. Attending and participating in events like farmers markets, trade shows, community yard sales and such, are great ways to get your name out there and help people to become more aware of you and your business.

Do your best not to tell yourself that you can't find prospects because you can! Take the time needed to evaluate your current routine. You will get noticed by stepping out and trying new things. If you do these three things you will have no issues being seen and finding prospects to grow your business. Now that you understand how to find prospects, it's important to weed out the good ones from the bad ones.

Types of Prospects

As you start focusing your efforts on finding, naturally you're going to have more people to talk with and more potential prospects interested in hearing what you have to say. The more people you talk with the more important it will become to determine who is truly interested and who is not. You'll need to identify where each individual lies on this spectrum so you know where to focus your time and efforts to see the best results. Let's discuss each of these different types of prospects:

- **Naysayers** - These individuals are easy to spot. Naysayers will clearly communicate disinterest with you from the beginning and will be adamant about it. Typically if you continue to push or pry, they will negatively respond or even ignore you. At times they might insult you or even your business. Don't let it get you down, keep going. At some point it's possible that they could be interested, but do not waste your time or efforts trying to force them into learning about your company when they have clearly said no. Your time and efforts will be best spent on more interested individuals. You can always leave them with an invitation to act and let them decide how to proceed.

> **Tip:** When you deal with these types of individuals do so tactfully and professionally. If they're not interested then move on. Don't take it as your responsibility to start an argument to prove or defend your company.

- **People Pleasers** - Have you ever spoken with someone who said yes to everything you had to say? Or someone who seemed to tell you everything they thought you wanted to hear? If you have, then you've experienced the frustration that comes when they give you false hope and ultimately don't ever act. I call these people pleasers. Now I'm not insulting these individuals because as humans we naturally want to please others and don't want to put ourselves or others in awkward situations. So typically we think it's easier to tell them what they want to hear instead of putting ourselves in a spot of saying no or having to potentially argue or prove our point. However, in your finding efforts it's better for someone to tell you they aren't interested than to have them say yes and nothing come of it. Identify the people pleasers in your prospecting efforts and don't waste your time on them. This will significantly free up time and reduce the frustration that happens when people are not progressing.

> **Tip:** Remember, even business builders can be people pleasers. Help your business builders feel comfortable and create an honest and open communication with them. By creating open communication you will see them open up and speak more about how they feel instead of just saying "yes".

- **Potentials (Fence Sitters)** - Potentials can be some of your best prospects. They are neither for your company nor against it, they are simply not sure. It's your job to help them, educate them, and ensure they understand the benefits of what your company could bring to their life. It's extra important to add value to these prospects and help them understand the benefits your company offers. It will be worth your time to work with and cultivate these individuals.

- **Interested Prospects** - Unlike your potentials, interested prospects have made the decision that they want to be involved with your company. However, they have something holding them back. This could be a spouse, an unsettled doubt, financial reasons or something else. So be sure that you're patient with them—guide and help them when needed. Don't forget to give them invitations to act and follow up with them regularly. In time these individuals can become loyal customers or strong business builders. Give them adequate support, but don't smother them.

- **Golden Prospects** - A golden prospect is someone who is interested, engaged, and truly wants to learn more about what you have to say. Golden prospects are eager to learn more and struggle waiting until the next interaction. They tell you yes because it's something they want, something they see that will make a difference in their life, and something that will impact them for good. These are the types of people you want to be working with and that will help you grow the business you want to grow. Find these golden prospects, help them grow, and you will as well.

It's important to follow a general rule of three contact points when working with all of the different types of prospects. From the initial time you talk with them give yourself three follow-up attempts. If they are not moving forward or progressing after these attempts, then you should move on. However, don't write them off completely. Keep them on your list of prospects and come back to them at a later date because sometimes timing is simply the issue for even your most golden of prospects.

> **Tip:** Remember not to take it personally when someone tells you no, and don't feel bad for taking them off your list of current prospects after three attempts. It's business, treat it that way and you'll see results.

Creating a Prospecting Outline

How many times have you thought that if you just had the perfect script you would be able to talk with everyone? Let me tell you something, that's simply not the case. You could use the same script as five other people and all have different results based off of your personalities and what comes natural to each of you. This is one of the biggest issues people have—they think they can use a set script and see huge results. However, the script is not natural for them and something they can't connect with. With the techniques listed below you will be able to create a prospecting outline that is natural for you, gets people interested in what you're saying, and is customized to your personality.

There are hundreds of personality tests out there and different ways to identify your unique characteristics and qualities. There are people who like to be in control, others who aim to please, people who want to know all the information and understand the details before they do anything, and still others who simply just want to have fun. It's important that you understand who you are as well as some of your strengths and weaknesses. However, equally as important you need to understand a bit about your prospect. As you strive to better understand their personality and customize your message in a way that speaks to them, they will become more open and receptive to what you have to say.

Tip: Remember your message is about the prospect and not about you. Customize your message to speak directly to them. Go with the flow of the conversation and don't be thrown off if they say or do something that takes you away from your "comfortable" message.

Keep in mind when talking with prospects and creating your outlines, it will be a bit different depending on if it's in person, online, or over the phone. Your goal will still be the same and you will include as much of the same information as possible. However, you want to keep it natural. Below are a few tips for talking with prospects over the phone and online:

Phone

- *Sound Busy* - Busy people are successful people. Don't get on the phone and shoot the breeze. Let them know you just have a few quick minutes, but you wanted to connect with them because what you have to share is *that* important.

- *Keep it Short* - Get to know and connect with them. Do everything like you always would, just keep it short and be respectful of their time. When prospecting, phone calls should be no more than a couple minutes long.

- *Follow Up* - Set a follow-up appointment with your prospects and be sure to give them a certain date and time. Again, you want to show you're busy. People automatically assume that busy people are successful and it builds a certain level of credibility.

Example: Hey Samantha! My name is Justin. Your friend Shellie told me that I should give you a call. I just have a couple minutes and wanted to talk to you briefly about a product both Shellie and I have been using. Has she told you much about it? Do you think it could benefit you? I know you're busy and so am I, but would you have time we could talk more about this and get to know each other a bit more later this week? Would Thursday before noon work?

Online

- *Connect* - You'll want to make a connection immediately when using social media, email, or any other online tool. Send them a message, and on the first point of contact, find common ground that you can build upon. If you don't connect, the chances of them responding back drop drastically.

- *Keep it Short* - Don't go into your life story. Keep it to the point and about them.

- *Respect Time* - We need to respect people's time, even on social media. Help them to see the value in what you have to say and show them you are respectful of what they have going on.

- *Follow Up* - Set a time and date to communicate with them in more detail over the phone.

  Example: Hey Thomas! I noticed you work as an entrepreneur. I am trying to get together with a group of like-minded people to see how we can help each other out and grow our businesses in the local community. Would you have time we could talk on Monday at 5:00pm to see if this might be something you would be interested in?

Don't make it about your business, but a way you could mutually grow together and benefit each other. This will make a huge difference in the way your message is received. Find a problem and give a solution. In the example above, it's all about growing each other's businesses and not about you, your company, or even the products or services. Focus on your prospects and you will be a success.

If a person needs to be in control, it's important to help them feel like they are in control. If they like to have fun then focus on the retreat trips your company offers or something that will connect with them in a fun way. If they like to please others then make sure they understand that you want them to do things that are best for them, that you're fine with whatever decision they make, and if they need more information to make a decision you will provide that for them. It's so easy to get caught up in a one-message-works-for-everyone mentality and that's simply not the case. Take the time to connect with your prospects and get to know them so you can create a message tailored to them. You will see a difference in your prospecting outlines if you follow these suggestions.

Now that we've discussed the importance of understanding your personality and the personality of your prospects, let's talk about the five steps that are important when creating an outline. Typically all prospecting outlines should include at least a small portion of each of the steps below. These five steps are meant to provide guidelines for you to follow when creating an outline that works:

1. **Introduction** - Introduce yourself and briefly get to know the person. This is not the time to word vomit on them about your company's products or services. Genuinely say hello and get to know them. This does not need to be a huge chunk of your outline and can be as simple as a greeting and a question or two.

2. **Connect** - When you're getting to know them, find something that helps you connect with them. This could be the fact that you have a child on the same sports team as theirs, that you live in the same neighborhood, or that you both use lemons from the produce section of your favorite store. Just find a way to connect with them. When creating your outline, you don't necessarily need to write this out, but make sure to leave time for it. I like to write a few questions down that I might ask and have them available if needed. Be flexible and allow yourself to connect.

3. **Message** - What is the point you want to address? What is it you want to leave them with? How can you add value to their

lives? Keep this simple. This is not the time to give them tons of information about your company. Sometimes you will connect with people and not even mention your business, and that's ok, as long as you have a way to continue connecting with them. The message needs to be natural and work for everyone involved.

4. **Invitation to Act** - This is the most important part of your outline. Make sure you have a clear invitation that works for them, something to get them to keep in touch, to meet up, to learn more, or whatever is natural. However, make sure the invitation is there and that it is super clear.

5. **Follow Up** - Make sure you have a way to follow up with them. Add them on Facebook, connect with them through email, send them a text message or something—just be sure to have a way to follow up and interact with them again.

The steps listed above will help you in creating your prospecting outlines. Instead of having a word-for-word script, these outlines should provide you with a list of talking points. Remember, they're used to help you get comfortable and to teach you the most important and basic items to discuss. Use the example outlines below to help you get started.

Three to Five Minute Example Outline

Introduction - Hey! Nice to meet you. I have noticed… (This is the time to find a way to get to know them. So if you're at a child's game and you see a parent that has been there several times, you might say something like, "I have noticed that you come to the baseball fields often. Do you have a child playing here as well?" Find a simple yet obvious way to get to know the person. If you're at a gas station, seriously be like, "Hey you use this gas station as well?" Of course they do, you're standing across from them, but it gets them talking. Don't overthink getting to know them and don't feel dumb if you ask a super obvious question.)

Connect - Take what you have learned about them and now connect with them. Relating back to the child's sports team example from above, say something like, "That's awesome you have a child playing as well! I think we played your team a few weeks back. How is the team doing?" (This is your opportunity to connect with them and find common ground. Have fun, don't make this rushed, and genuinely connect.)

Message - Here is your time to simply share something quick and short, but effective to help them know what you have to offer. Again, back to our example from above, share something like, "I love having my kid playing sports, but it can get quite tiring at times. I'm sure you know all about that. I have come to rely on this product to get me through the long days, it makes such a difference!"

Invitation to Act - Take the time to give a simple and natural invitation. Using the same example, try something like, "Take this sample and try it. The next time you come to the ball park, seriously you will see a huge difference. It is amazing what it has done for me and sometimes it's the only way I can make it the entire day!"

Follow Up - Finally make sure you have a way to contact them. Back to our example, use something like this, "My number is attached to the back. If you like it and want more information, don't hesitate to ask me. Would you mind if I added you to one of my pages on Facebook? I would love to get your honest feedback about the product on this page once you have tried it."

If time permits, go back into talking about sports and your kids. Keep it super simple and when creating outlines, follow the example above.

30-Second Example Outline

The example below is a script of what I would say if I had only 30 seconds to talk with someone. When creating your outlines for this script simply create talking points and ways to give yourself ideas. You only have 30 seconds so you don't need to add tons.

"Hey! So nice to meet you! I noticed we both are here often. It's crazy

77

the things we do for our kids. This is the only way I can do it! This product saves me! Here take this, it's an extra. And trust me, from one parent to another, you will see the difference. I will find you next week and want to hear how you felt after giving it a try! Have a great night."

Over the next 60 days, you will have the opportunity to create many outlines, so stay focused and follow the 60-day plan. You'll be surprised because the more you practice these, the less you will rely on them. These steps can be used for both a three to five-minute or a thirty-second prospecting outline. The main goal is to present yourself, invite them, and have a way to follow up.

> **Tip:** Outlines are simply talking points that allow you to introduce yourself and get to know the prospect, to connect with them, share a brief message, leave them with an invitation to act, and have a way to follow up with them again. Don't stress about having every word or every exact detail for your outline—simply create talking points, practice them, and be natural about it.

60-Day Prospecting Plan

Now that we have discussed the dos and don'ts of prospecting, it's time to get to work. The 60-day plan is designed to help you build confidence in your prospecting abilities, have you talking to people each day, and help you create prospecting outlines that work so you will see results. Master the art of prospecting by implementing the 60-day plan. Give it your all and this will become one of your biggest strengths.

> **Tip:** Get your team doing the 60-day Prospecting Plan with you. Learn, grow, and succeed together. For additional resources, use the First Steps to the Summit booklet to get you and your team started at prospecting.

The first 30 days of the prospecting plan are designed to get you talking to people and creating solid prospecting outlines that work. By the end of the first 30 days, you will have talked with 108 people, created 20 prospecting outlines, and made a difference in your business! The first 30 days are oftentimes the most difficult because they really get you out of your comfort zone—but this will teach you things about yourself. No matter how hard it gets or seems, keep with it, stay strong, and make it happen! Let's get to work!

> **Tip:** Sometimes finding an accountability partner is a good idea when tackling a new plan like this. Find someone that will help you stay accountable and get things done. No excuses, you got this!

Day 1

1. Identify what you like about prospecting. Do you find it fun, exciting, etc.? Even if you don't like prospecting, pick one thing you like about it—even if this is just to simply grow your business, just pick something.

2. Identify what stops you from talking to people or prospecting. What are you afraid of? What don't you like about it and what obstacles stand in your way? Write these down in a place you can have them readily available. We will come back to these multiple times over the next month.

3. Create five prospecting outlines that help you talk for three to five minutes about your company's products or services and keep them with you at all times. You never know when you will find someone to talk to—and until you master prospecting, these outlines will help you out immensely!

Day 2

1. Practice your five product or service outlines. Get so comfortable with them, that you know them backwards and forwards to really understand what it is you're saying.

2. Create a follow-up system. It does not matter how you create this, just make sure you keep track of all the prospects you will be talking with by getting their name, email, and phone number when possible. Make sure you have a place to take a few notes about the prospect so you can easily remember them and connect again when following up.

3. Today we will start small. Talk with two new prospects. Use the outlines we have created and put them to practice. Don't be nervous, you will make mistakes, and that's ok. Just remember at the end of the 60 days you will be a master of prospecting.

> **Tip:** We live in a world where it is super easy to find people to talk to. Many people can be found online—and you will always find people in any public place that you go. Just make sure you're finding and talking with *new* people.

Day 3

1. Time to evaluate your outlines. How did the conversations from yesterday go? How did you do? How did the outlines work? What do you need to change?

2. Pick one issue from yesterday's conversation and fix it. Tweak your outline, work on your confidence, or whatever needs improvement. Simply pick one item and make it better.

3. Use your newly updated outlines and talk with five people. Practice, practice, and practice some more.

Day 4

1. Practice your five outlines with a friend or family member. Get their opinion and feedback.

2. Make appropriate changes to your outlines. Use the feedback you received to improve your outlines.

3. Use your newly updated outlines and talk with two new prospects.

Day 5

1. Take ten minutes and revise your outlines again. Use the feedback from yesterday's interactions to improve your outlines.

2. Use your newly updated outlines and talk with five new prospects.

Day 6

1. Make any needed changes to your outlines. By now you should have five product or service outlines that you like and are comfortable with.

2. Practice your outlines for fifteen minutes.

3. Put your outlines away and relax. Let your mind rest. Tomorrow is going to be a big day!

Day 7

1. Now that you have five revised product or service outlines, it's time to really put them to work. Today you will talk to ten new prospects. Be calm and have fun with it! You're growing one step closer to a million dollar business every time you talk with someone.

Day 8

1. Take 20 minutes and think about your "why". Remember what motivates you to do hard things. Prospecting can be hard by itself and following a plan like this will test your limits and stretch you in multiple ways. Remembering your "why" will keep you focused and motivated to move forward, even on the hard days.

2. Create five prospecting outlines that will help you talk for three to five minutes about your company's business opportunity and keep them with you at all times. You never know when you will find someone to talk to—and until you master prospecting, these outlines will help you out immensely!

 Reference: Please see the Self Development chapter in this book for more information on your "why".

Day 9

1. Practice your five business opportunity outlines. Get so comfortable with them that you know them backwards and forwards, and understand what it is you're saying.

2. Like last week, we will start small. Talk with two new prospects today. Use the outlines we have created and put them to practice.

Day 10

1. Time to evaluate your outlines. How did the interactions from yesterday go? How did you do? How did the outlines work? What do you need to change?

2. Pick one issue from yesterday's conversation and fix it. Tweak your outline, work on your confidence, or whatever needs improvement. Simply pick one item and get started making improvements.

3. Use your newly updated outlines and talk with five new prospects! The more you practice the easier it gets.

Day 11

1. Practice your five outlines with a friend or family member. Get their opinion and feedback.

2. Make appropriate changes to your outlines. Use the feedback you received to improve your outlines.

3. Use your newly updated outlines and talk with two new prospects.

Day 12

1. Take ten minutes and revise your outlines. Use the feedback from yesterday's interactions to improve your outlines.

2. Use your newly updated outlines and talk with five new prospects.

Day 13

1. Make any final changes to your outlines. By now you should have five

business opportunity outlines that you like and are comfortable with.

2. Practice your outlines for 15 minutes.

3. Put your outlines away and relax. Let your mind rest. Tomorrow is going to be another big day!

Day 14

1. Now that you have five revised business opportunity outlines, it's time to put them to work. Today you will talk to ten new prospects. This is no different than what you did last week, you'll just be using different outlines.

Day 15

1. Create five 30-second outlines about your products or services. The goal of these outlines is to help you deliver your message in a short amount of time. Make sure you capture the most important information and facts your prospect would need to hear. This is not the time for a ton of information, just keep it simple and precise.

2. Practice your 30-second outlines with a friend or family member. Get feedback and input from them.

Day 16

1. Practice your five new outlines. Get comfortable with them, know them, and really practice them. Tweak what needs to be changed.

2. Talk to five new prospects using your newly revised 30-second outlines.

Day 17

1. Take ten minutes and evaluate how you did with your outlines. How did your conversations go yesterday? How did people receive your message? How do you feel about the outlines?

2. Pick one area from the evaluation in which you can improve. Focus on it, tweak it, and then master it.

3. Talk to five new prospects today using your 30-second outlines. Remember, practice, practice, and practice some more.

Day 18

1. Revise your 30-second outlines after yesterday's interactions. What worked and what did not?

2. Practice your newly revised outlines with a friend or family member. Get their feedback and make needed changes.

3. Talk to five new prospects using your newest 30-second outlines.

Day 19

1. Pick two concerns from yesterday's interactions and tweak them. Make the needed changes and perfect your outlines.

2. Evaluate yourself. How have you changed since starting the 60-day plan? Are you starting to feel more comfortable? What don't you like about prospecting? What do you like about it now? Compare your answers with those you did on day one.

3. Talk to five new prospects today using your newly revised outlines.

Day 20

1. Identify your biggest strength and weakness from yesterday's evaluation. Set three action items to help you improve your weakness.

2. Take a look at your 30-second outlines and make any needed changes.

3. Take 20 minutes and practice your newly revised outlines.

4. Take a break and relax. You will need it!

Day 21

1. Now that you have five perfected outlines, it's time to really put them to work. Today you will talk to ten new prospects. Remember to keep it short and make these count!

Day 22

1. Create five 30-second outlines about your business opportunity. These are just like the 30-second product or service outlines that you created last week, but simply replaced with your business opportunity.

2. Practice your 30-second outlines with a friend or family member. Get feedback and input from them.

Day 23

1. Practice your five outlines—get comfortable with them, know them, and really practice them. Tweak what needs to be changed.

2. Talk to five new prospects using your newly revised 30-second outlines.

Day 24

1. Take ten minutes and evaluate your outlines. How did your conversations go yesterday? How did people receive your message? How do you feel about the outlines?

2. Pick one area from the evaluation in which you could improve, focus on it, tweak it, and then master it.

3. Talk to five new prospects today using your 30-second outlines. You're almost halfway through the 60-day Prospecting Plan. Keep going!

Day 25

1. Revise your 30-second outlines after yesterday's interactions. What worked and what did not?

2. Practice your newly revised outlines with a friend or family member. Get their feedback and make needed changes.

3. Talk to five new prospects using your newest 30-second outlines.

Day 26

1. Pick two concerns from yesterday's interactions and tweak them. Make the needed changes and perfect your outlines.

2. Talk to five new prospects today using your newest outlines.

Day 27

1. Take a look at your 30-second outlines and make any needed changes.

2. Take 20 minutes and practice your newly revised outlines.

3. Take a break and relax.

Day 28

1. Now that you have five new outlines, it's time to put them to work. Today you will talk to ten new prospects. Keep it short, stay focused, and have fun!

Days 29 and 30

1. Take the next two days and enjoy yourself. Take a brief break from prospecting.

Take a moment and pat yourself on the back! You have completed the first 30 days of the prospecting plan. Over the next 30 days we will be using the outlines we created and the skills that you've developed to follow up with the prospects from the first 30 days—and you'll be talking with over 140 people!

Now that we have developed outlines that work, we are going to change them up. We will be using creative strategies and techniques to make your outlines flexible and guaranteed to work in all situations, as well as helping you become comfortable talking with people and prospecting without relying solely on your outlines.

Day 31

1. Take 20 minutes to evaluate the success of your first 30 days. How did it go? What did you do well? What could you do better? What have you learned since starting?

2. Talk to five new prospects using any of your outlines. Decide which one you're most comfortable with and use it.

Day 32

1. Take 20 minutes to think about your invitation to act. Are you giving a clear invitation when talking with prospects? Do they know exactly what it is you're asking them to do? If not, take a few minutes and tweak your outlines to reflect a clear invitation to act.

2. Follow up with your prospects from days 1-15. Check in on them and make sure things are going well, ask them about the invitation you extended, and be sure to extend a second one.

3. Talk to ten new prospects using your 30-second product or service outline.

Day 33

1. Spend 30 minutes updating your list of places and ideas to find new prospects.

2. Talk to five new prospects using your business opportunity outlines.

Day 34

1. Take 15 minutes to evaluate your body language. What are you communicating to people when you're talking to them? How is your message received?

2. Talk to ten new prospects using your 30-second business opportunity outline.

Day 35

1. Talk to five new prospects using any of your outlines. Today when

you're talking with them, pay close attention to their body language and mannerisms. Are they open to receiving your message, or are they closed off and just hearing what you have to say?

Day 36

1. How are people responding to your questions and invitations? Are you getting clear answers? Are you seeing results from them when you follow up? Take a few minutes and think about the last several weeks and the reactions you have been receiving. Tweak the things you can on your part to get better results.

2. Talk to six new prospects using any of your outlines.

Day 37

1. Pick three ways you can present yourself better and have better body language. Use your evaluation from day 34 and really focus on these things when talking with people.

2. Talk to seven new prospects using an outline of your choice. Remember to pick an outline you're comfortable with, but also change it up so you improve at all of them.

Day 38

1. Identify one business builder who is interested in learning more about prospecting. Take 15 minutes to teach them some of the things you have learned and then answer their questions. You will become better at prospecting as you start teaching others.

2. Take your business builder prospecting with you and talk to ten new prospects. You can pick the outline, but be sure to get feedback from your business builder and answer any questions they may have.

Day 39

1. Practice prospecting with your business builder. Take turns being the prospect. This is a great time to show them what you have learned and to help them see that they too can become an expert at prospecting.

2. Talk to five new prospects using your product or service outlines.

Day 40

1. Follow up with prospects from days 16-30.

2. Talk to five new prospects using your business opportunity outlines.

Day 41

1. Take ten minutes to evaluate your passion for prospecting. What changes have you seen since you started the 60-day Prospecting Plan? Are you feeling more eager and confident to talk with people? Keep these answers close by and look at them on days that seem hard. You should be seeing huge progress by now.

2. Talk to ten new prospects using your 30-second product or service outlines.

Day 42

1. Have your business builder become the teacher and teach you what they have learned about prospecting. Help them when they get stuck and assist them in mastering the principles needed to become a master prospector.

2. Talk to ten new prospects using your 30-second business opportunity outlines.

Day 43

1. Free day! Take some time away from prospecting, you deserve it.

Day 44

Talk to 20 new prospects using any of your outlines! Stretch yourself, you can do this!

Day 45

1. Identify three to five things you like most about each outline. Over the next several days you will begin prospecting without relying so heavily on your outlines.

2. Talk to ten new prospects. Remember not to rely so heavily on your outlines and simply use the skills you have acquired and talk with people. Use the techniques you have learned to start to talk to prospects without your outlines.

> **Tip:** Remember your outlines are guides to get you started, to help you focus on the needed topics of discussion, and to help you build confidence. Now that you know the flow and how it feels to prospect, you don't need these as much. Stay confident and apply what you know.

Day 46

1. Spend 30 minutes with your business builder to practice resolving doubts and concerns. Simply present your company and have them question you, tell you "no", or anything to throw you off your routine. Now resolve these concerns! Have fun with this. It will teach you how to resolve concerns on the fly when you're out prospecting.

2. Talk to 15 new prospects.

Day 47

1. Free day! The next four days will be pretty intense. Get ready—you will do great!

Day 48

1. Talk to 25 new prospects.

2. Follow up with prospects from days 30-45.

Day 49

1. Talk to 15 new prospects.

Day 50

1. Talk to 20 new prospects.

Day 51

1. Free day! Enjoy a brief break. Get ready for what's to come over the next few days.

Day 52

1. Have some fun with prospecting. Pick a list of ten random words and use these when you're out prospecting. This exercise may seem a bit crazy, but it will help you be able to talk to anyone about anything.

2. Talk to ten new prospects.

Day 53

1. Talk to 15 new prospects.

Day 54

1. Talk to 20 new prospects.

Day 55

1. Talk to 25 new prospects.

Day 56

1. Take the day off from prospecting. The last few days are going to be intense.

Day 57

1. Talk to 30 new prospects.

Day 58

1. Talk to 35 new prospects.

Day 59

1. Talk to 40 new prospects.

Day 60

1. Talk to 50 new prospects.

2. One week from today follow up with the prospects from days 45-60.

> **Tip:** Remember we live in a world where prospecting can be done in person as well as over the Internet. Get creative, talk with people, and pace yourself. As you pace yourself, you will be surprised how simple it might be to talk to 50 prospects in one day.

By the end of 60 days you will have completely mastered the concepts of prospecting. You will have created outlines, worked on ideas for finding, taught others how to prospect, and mastered the topic to the point of not even needing your outlines. You should be able to overcome obstacles, give a clear invitation, and more than anything, you will have talked with people and grown your business. Use this plan to help people on your team master the technique of prospecting, and when you feel stuck, tired, or like you don't have prospects to talk with, start the prospecting plan again.

Timing is Everything

As it relates to prospecting, it is also important to talk about timing. Sadly, no matter how many prospects we talk to it is unlikely they will all say yes, seem interested, or even talk with us. Guess what? That's ok! The biggest thing to remember when growing your business is that timing is not about us, but has everything to do with when your prospects are ready and when the timing works best for them.

I remember when I started my business—wow, was I excited! I wanted and needed things to happen quickly and to grow fast. I found myself talking to everyone and just knew that they would be interested. I soon came to the realization that my eagerness did not translate to the same eagerness for them. This was not only the case with my prospects, but also with my customers and business builders. I had huge goals for the team, high expectations, and I assumed that everyone else shared these same goals and ambitions with me.

Many times they would agree with my message, get excited when we talked, and then later in the week when we'd touch base, nothing had been done. Remember to be eager and excited, but don't follow my example and push your timing onto others. When things started happening more naturally, my business grew. My team was not only excited, but worked together more closely—and this cohesive teamwork is a necessity in the industry.

Set goals, talk to everyone, but at the end of the day don't forget it's not about *your* timing, it is about *their* timing and it's important to let things pan out naturally. When the timing is correct things will work out for the best. When people say no, it's not always a reflection of you and the things you're saying, so keep a positive attitude and remember the timing is theirs.

Tip: When you talk to someone, always write it down. Keep track of their information and don't assume a "no" means forever. Remember, timing is everything, so keep following up with them regularly.

Follow Up

Talking with people is key, but the follow up is just as important. I can't even begin to tell you how many people I have talked with and never got their information, never followed up with them, or unfortunately forgot about them. You never know who might become your best customer or your most successful business builder, so everyone needs to be followed up with and given the opportunity to progress.

Keep track of the people you talk with. Record some basic information about them to help you remember who they are and what you discussed. Add them to your "prospecting email list" and send them a weekly email for ten weeks after initial contact. The goal of these emails is to educate, remind them of who you are, what you do, and what benefits are waiting for them once they decide to move forward. I focus these emails on potential customers—if they are interested in the business opportunity I let that come later—but the focus should be on the product or service offered by your company and exactly what they need to do to become a customer.

> **Tip:** Subject lines are everything in these emails. Use something that gets their attention, makes them excited to open it, and help them remember who you are. Don't make your subject line seem like you're trying to sell them something.

Basic Email Structure

- **Greeting** - Simply greet them and remind them who you are. Thank them for taking the time to get to know you and let them know that you're excited to help them learn more about you and your company. Follow up on your previous week's invitation to act.

- **Announcements** - Share with them exciting news about your company. Make these items super clear, easy to understand, and to the point. Your goal should be to give them as much information as possible using the least amount of text. You need to capture their attention to guarantee they continue reading.

- **Invitation** - Invite them to learn more, take the next step, ask questions, or to purchase. Make sure the invitation is clear and to the point, something they can easily accomplish.

- **Farewell** - End the email, thank them for their time, and leave them excited and ready for next week's communication.

Email 1: *Remember Me* - The entire goal of this email is to touch base and remind them who you are and what you do. Thank them for their time and make sure they know how to contact you with any questions or concerns.

Example:

Hey! Here is the email I told you I would be sending—I hope it finds you well. Like I mentioned before, I am with [your company name] and I love what I do! I am so excited to share a bit more information with you about my company and why I love it so much. I know you're going to love it!

I wanted to make sure you had the information needed to get in contact with me if you have any questions or if I can help you out in any way.

Take some time this week to research a bit about the company and let me know if you have questions.

Look forward to getting to know you better! Have a great week!

[Your name]

Email 2: *Guess What?* - Find something special and exciting to share with them. This can be something basic about your company. Remember, it's new for them, but it will help them learn more about what you do.

Example:

Hey! I hope you had a great week! Did you have time to check out the company website? What did you think? Remember, if you have questions, don't hesitate to let me know.

Guess what? [your company name] is:
- [List out three to five bulleted points that make your company special. Make this something that they can relate with and understand.]

Enjoy the rest of your week and take some time to think about these amazing things we discussed tonight and let me know if you have questions.

[Your name]

Email 3: *Did You Know?* - This is like the previous email—just with a different title and a different way to educate them. Teach them something they may have not known about your company.

Example:

Happy Monday! I hope you had a great weekend and that you enjoyed some of the interesting items we discussed last week.

Did you know [your company name] offers:
- [Give them three to five bulleted items about your company]

Take time to think about these this week. Can you see the benefits of having a company like this in your life?

Have a great week!

[Your name]

Email 4: *Wow, I Can't Believe This!* - This is the time to blow their socks off. Tell them about an amazing promotion, something exciting going on, or maybe your enrollment package. It just needs to be something to make them think twice about the deal they would be getting if they choose to become a customer.

Example:

Hey! I hope your week was great and that you had time to research a bit more about what we discussed last week.

I am so excited to share something with you that I simply can't believe. I am always amazed about great deals and promotions, but I think this tops them all! [Tell them about a promotion you or your company are offering.]

Now is the time to get started and to take advantage of this amazing promotion. When can we talk to get you started?

Have a great week!

[Your name]

Email 5: *Recovery* - Have fun with this email. This is basically to reiterate the promotion from the email above. You want them to think that it was so amazing that even you are *still* shocked by it a week later. Educate and help them to really see the value of this promotion.

Example:

Another week has come and gone and I have to tell you that I am still excited about last week's amazing promotion. People have been taking advantage of it all week and it truly is amazing!

Have you had time to think more about it? Let's get on the phone and get you started ASAP. If you have already taken advantage of

this great promotion, how are you enjoying it?
Have a wonderful week!

[Your name]

Email 6: *What's Stopping You?* - Ask them what's holding them back from moving forward. Remind them of some of the great things you have to offer and get them thinking about what's stopping them from moving forward.

Example:

Hey! I hope you had another amazing week!

So what's stopping you? What's holding you back from making the decision to change your life and start on a new path? Think about it, what do you have to lose?

If you need anything let me know, have a great week!

[Your name]

Email 7: *It's as Easy as 1, 2 , 3* - Show them how easy it is to become a customer in three simple steps. Make the process super simple and not complicated. Your three steps need to be something they can look at and accomplish within in a few minutes.

Example:

Hey! I hope this email finds you well. Have you had time to think about the great promotion and to decide if you're interested in moving forward?

I simply wanted to let you know how easy it is to get started when you're ready.

- [List out three steps for them to become a customer. Keep them simple and clear.]

[Your name]

Email 8: *Again, I am shocked!* - This is the time to talk to them about another amazing deal or promotion. Get them excited, and let them know that being a customer is rewarding and you will always be looking out for them and getting them the best promotions possible.

Example:

Happy Day! Another great week! Hopefully you found the steps in last week's email helpful and something to have on hand when you're ready to get started.

I am constantly shocked by this company's generous offers. They are currently offering [Provide them more promotions or inform them of things going on. Help them to see how great a benefit this really is for them.]

Let me know if you're interested in learning more about this amazing promotion. Have a great week!

[Your name]

Email 9: *Check This Out!* This is all about focusing on one of your popular products or services. Educate them briefly on this item and help them to see the benefits and impact it could have on their life.

Example:

Hey!

I hope you had another good week. What did you think of that amazing promotion last week? Seriously, I can't believe it!

This week I want to talk a bit about one of our top [products or services] (Be sure to go into detail about this item and help them see why it is so great. Remember to keep it short).

Let me know if you would like to learn more or to give this a try. Have a great week!

[Your name]

Email 10: *See You On the Other Side* - Thank them for their time and interest and let them know you're excited to continue helping them as a customer. Remind them of how to get in contact with you if they have any questions.

Example:

Hey! It's hard to believe it has been over two months since we first met! I hope you have enjoyed learning a bit more about what I do and why I am so passionate about this company.

Just know I am here if you need anything and am excited to help you. Take advantage of some of the great promotions we have going on and let me know how I can help!

Have a great week!

[Your name]

Tip: Keep email laws in mind. It's important for a person to have the option to opt out of receiving future emails from you. And once they have opted out, you *need* to ensure they don't receive further communications from you.

Once they become a customer or business builder, be sure to switch them over from your prospecting list to one of your educational email lists. At the end of the ten emails, if the prospect still hasn't become a customer, don't give up yet. Apply the three follow up attempt rule. If they don't respond after three attempts, then move on. Don't waste time on a non-responsive prospect.

Prospecting with a Facebook Business Page

Facebook business pages are a great way to educate existing prospects and to find new ones. This is a public page on Facebook designed to educate on your products or services, promote your company, and add value to prospects' lives. Focus on educating and inviting instead of pushing the sale or getting your prospects to purchase. As you educate, connect, and have impact on your prospects' lives, they will naturally purchase.

Tip: Invite your team to participate on this page and encourage them to invite their prospects. The goal is to create a community of interested prospects who, over time, will become customers or business builders.

I use the 85/15 rule for my posts—85% of the time my posts are all about education and value, while 15% of the time my posts are focused on the business or purchasing a product or service and are sales-focused. Posts should occur three times a day on weekdays and once a day on Saturday and Sunday. Remember, Facebook is not the place to be the pushy salesperson, so be smart with these posts. By being genuine, prospects will be able to relate to you and you will see good results come from it.

Follow the weekly schedule listed below as a template for your public Facebook page:

Monday

Post 1: Inspiration and Motivation - Keep this post simple. Post an inspirational quote or video that motivates, uplifts, and inspires people. People enjoy posts that will help them feel important and stay positive. These simple quotes or videos can go a long way.

Example Post:

1. "To succeed in life, you need three things: a wishbone, a backbone, and a funny bone." - Reba McEntire

Post 2: What Makes Your Company Special - Provide facts about your company, what they do, why they do it, and what makes the company great. Show and share how the company has impacted you in your life. It is so important to focus on how great your company is and delivering it in a fun, factual way.

Example Posts:

1. Did you know [your company name] is one of the only companies that does [insert unique thing your company does]? What an amazing opportunity we have to use these great products or services!

2. Because of [product or service] my life has improved drastically. I now can take a bit more time to enjoy my family while resting assured that [an aspect of your life] has improved.

Post 3: Weekly Featured Product or Service - Pick a new product or service and educate others about it, teach them how to use it, and show fun ways you have used or applied it in your life. This is *not* a sales post, but simply a way to educate and create interest.

Example Post:

1. I'm excited to announce this week's product or service! We will be talking about [give some detailed information about it and how it can be used].

Tuesday

Post 1: Did You Know? - These are some of my favorite posts and they can generate significant interaction. They're a great way to answer common questions or educate on facts about a product or service, and your company.

Example Post:

1. Did you know [provide a fun fact about your company, or one of its products or services]?

Post 2: Promotions and Incentives - This will be your first sales post. Talk about the promotions from your company, or maybe a promotion you currently have going on with your customers. Simply give an invite to try them out or ask questions. Remember to be natural and to extend a simple invitation to act. Be creative with this post and make it different each week.

Example Post:

1. Check out this amazing deal! This week only, take advantage of a great buy-one-get-one special. Purchase this amazing item and get an extra one to use as a gift or stash away for a rainy day.

Post 3: Product or Service in Action - Show your company's products or services in action and help people see how to apply them in their daily lives. Use the product or service from the promotion above for this post.

Example Post:

1. Not only can you get two of [product] for the price of one, but did you know it can also be used for [specific use]?

Wednesday

Post 1: Did You Know? - Follow the same instructions on Tuesday's post.

Post 2: Inspiration and Motivation - Follow the same instructions on Monday's post.

Post 3: Fun Facts - Provide creative ideas, uses, or fun facts that help them better understand your company or how to implement its products or services in their life.

Example Posts:

1. Have you tried [product] in your morning routine?

2. Taking time to use [service] will drastically save you time and allow you more time for those things you love most!

Thursday

Post 1: Get Personal - Have fun with this post. Share a bit about yourself, your story, why you are involved with your company, a hobby, or just anything fun. Help your prospects get to know you better and feel comfortable working with you.

Example Post:

1. Five years ago today I started my journey with [your company]. Looking back, there have been ups and downs in my life. However, [your company] has been one that's remained constant. The benefits [company] brings to my life are huge! I am so thankful I became a customer.

Post 2: Product or Service in Action - Follow the same instructions on Tuesday's post.

Post 3: Product Invitation - Invite others to try a product, give feedback on something they have tried, or reach out with questions. Again, this needs to be a soft approach and something natural and casual, not pushy. This is your second sales post.

Examples Posts:

1. Have you had the opportunity to try this week's promotion? Take advantage of this great opportunity and try one of our most popular products or services.

2. What's stopping you from trying one of our many great products or services? Let me know if you have questions or if you're interested in trying something out!

Friday

Post 1: What Good Comes from Your Company - Share more about your company's differences and unique qualities.

Example Posts:

1. One of the great things about [your company] is they take a portion from every sale and give back to charities! Not only can you benefit from a great company, so can so many others!

2. [Your company] has spent years researching and understanding the industry. For this reason they have been rated number one in the industry for [specific reason].

Post 2: Relax and Enjoy the Weekend - Wish everyone a happy weekend. Use images that show how you use your company's products or services on your weekends. People associate the weekends with fun and freedom and this post should reflect that.

Example Post:

1. TGIF! Have any fun plans for the weekend? Take some time and spend it doing something fun! Check out the pictures of a typical weekend at my house!

Post 3: Making a Connection - This is your third and final sales post for the week. Get them thinking about what the company could do for them, how they could benefit from the product, and how they plan to use your products or services.

Example Posts:

1. What product or service do you think you could use most?

2. What benefits will this amazing company add to your life?

Saturday

Post 1: Inspiration and Motivation - Follow the same instructions in Monday's post.

Sunday

Post 1: Give Back or Contribute - Share examples of you or your company giving back. It should be something you enjoy doing, or something more personal about you, the company, or your team that people can relate to.

Example Post:

1. This week we had the opportunity to volunteer at a local food bank. One of the reasons I started working with [company] was to be able to give back to my local community. So thankful for the opportunities this brings into my life!

Tip: Along with the suggested material for each post, add an engaging photo to enhance the text.

Keep in mind these emails and posts are simply examples. Change them to fit your personality. Remember to keep them short, to the point, and get them to act. Oftentimes prospecting is not easy to master and for most it's something they're not comfortable with. Review this section over and over again, change your attitude and commit to being a professional prospector. Once you master prospecting, your business will climb to new heights.

To Do List

☐ Find three ways to connect with your company's products or services

☐ Evaluate your daily routine

☐ Find three new places you could work (coffee shops, libraries, etc.)

☐ Determine if your prospects are naysayers, people pleasers, potentials, interested prospects, or golden prospects

☐ Clear your mind, take a break, and relax before starting the 60-day Prospecting Plan

☐ Start the 60-day Prospecting Plan

☐ Create a prospecting follow up document

☐ Create emails for your "prospecting email list"

Tip: To learn more, follow me at facebook.com/trainwithjustin

Chapter Notes

Chapter 4
Sales

I would be lying if I said I was not excited to talk about sales! This is absolutely one of my favorite parts about the industry and something that changes our businesses on a daily basis if we are smart and work hard. When I was five, I went to my grandfather and asked him for a small business loan of a hundred dollars so I could open my own ice cream and candy business. I created a business plan and told him that I would go door to door to sell candy and ice cream to the neighbors— and that's what I did. I sold ice cream and candy like crazy and I paid the loan off in four days! I remember one day I was so stoked because I earned over $150! There was nothing I could not sell and the fun part about it was that I was making friends. I got to know new people and really enjoyed what I did. Looking back over my life, I realize I have always been a salesperson and have really enjoyed it. I look forward to the opportunity to get in front of people and tell them how I can help them live better lives.

Now, as sad as it is for me to realize this, I understand this is not the way most people feel about sales. Honestly, this is hands down the hardest area to master for most people within the industry. How many times have you said things like, "I am not a salesperson—I simply share", "I don't like salespeople either, I just love what I do and love helping people", or anything similar to fool yourself into doing sales? When I hear this, it makes me go a bit crazy inside. I want to scream out and remind each and everyone of you that you are a salesperson and that you're in the industry of sales. There are no ifs, ands, or buts about it. We are responsible for selling our company's products or services. When we do that, they pay us a commission—that, my friend, is sales. Now, before you go crazy inside, or think that I am crazy, let's identify why this is and why most people want the benefits of being a salesperson without being a salesperson.

Oftentimes we associate salespeople with being dishonest, overly pushy, inconsiderate, or only motivated by making a commission. Although I love sales and consider myself a salesperson, I still feel this way about so many within the industry. It's so frustrating to deal with someone that has only *their* best interests in mind, who pushes something that I don't really need or care about, who doesn't care about what I have to say, or that just keeps pushing their agenda. These individuals focus so much on the price, the incentives they receive from their company, or driving the nicest cars, that they don't care at all about their customers. When I see this happening, I cringe a bit inside because not only do I think this salesperson is stupid, but I also think that they really are hurting the industry for the rest of us.

Although there are people like this, there is great news—we can change the industry! There are ways you can be a salesperson while making a difference in someone's life and helping them receive products or services they really want and need. My goal is to be able to help you stand tall and join the army of honest, well-educated, supportive, motivated, and respected salespeople. I am confident that as you embrace the qualities and techniques discussed in this chapter, you will be happy to be a salesperson, and, as we work on these things together, we can change the industry and the way salespeople are seen. Commit today to be honest that you are a salesperson and you can change people's lives!

Now that you're excited, committed, and focused on being a better salesperson by changing the view others have of the industry, let's talk about what it takes to be successful at sales. If you can focus on these four items and let them guide your interactions with others, this will make the difference between you and the poor salespeople previously discussed. You will find that your interactions will be quite opposite compared to the negative interactions you may have had in the past.

1. **Making Connections Through Asking Questions** - Get your prospects to open up to and connect with you—this is done by asking questions. People want to be heard—they want to talk about and discuss what's going on in their lives. By allowing them to answer questions and talk about their lives, it will help them to feel more comfortable and minimize the feeling of being pressured to purchase something.

    Naturally we are guarded, we don't want to be told what to do, and we don't want to feel pressured to spend our hard-earned money on something we don't feel like we want or need. As we ask questions we are helping to get past the way these people feel, we are connecting with them, letting them know that we too are human, and that we really get what it is they are feeling. Once someone feels you care enough to connect they become much more open to hearing what you have to say and working with you. People are like onions, especially in a sales situation, you really have to peel them back layer by layer until they open up and are comfortable with you and what you're saying.

For a few minutes stop focusing on the sale or pushing your product or service and get to know your prospect. Try to relate with them and understand what they are going through. This step may seem like a waste of time or like something that really does not help generate volume. However, this is the best thing you can do. Truly get to know your prospect, understand and relate with them, and you will see a difference.

As you genuinely show interest in their life, you will see the sales process begins to happen much more naturally. They will ask you questions, they will show interest in what you do, and they will give you the chance to share your company with them. There is nothing better than telling someone about what you do and why you do it, knowing they really have interest and want to know.

2. **Offer Suggestions** - Once you have gained your prospect's trust by asking them questions and getting to know them, it is time to make some suggestions, give them ideas, or provide ways for them to implement your company in their life. You want them to make connections between what you are sharing and how it will personally benefit them. For example, "Would it be ok if I suggest something that may make you some extra money?" or "Could I make a small recommendation about a product or service that has changed my life and could really help you?" Make sure to keep it simple. You don't want to overwhelm them with your ideas or suggestions.

3. **Ease Up On the Control** - One of the biggest problems I see salespeople face is that they want to be in control of every situation all of the time. It is important to guide your prospect through the sales process, help them understand what you do, and to get them to act. However, you don't need to be in control the entire time. Let your prospects do most of the talking—and when I say most, I mean at least 70% of the talking. If they talk, ask questions—and just by guiding the conversation from time to time, you will see much more success.

The more they talk and open up the more success you will have. The key here is to remember it's about *them* and not *you*. The biggest issue we have with salespeople is how we feel after interacting with them—and that's because they make every situation about them and try to control everything that happens. Guess what? No one likes that—ease up on the control and let them give you the information you need to help them.

> **Tip:** Not sure if you struggle with control? Take time to think about some of these questions. Are you constantly thinking about what to say next, how to answer their questions, or what product or service you are going to present next? Are you telling them what they need, or convinced in your mind that they really need something, no matter what they are saying? Do you interrupt what they are saying because you know best? These are just a few signs that you might need to ease up a bit on the control. I know this can be hard, but surprisingly people do best when they can control their own life. You simply have to guide them to make connections between their life and your company.

4. **Clear Invitation** - This is absolutely the most important part of being a success at sales. Asking all of the questions, taking the time to understand and connect, and letting your prospect do most of the talking means nothing if there is not a clear and simple invitation to act. With a clear invitation you are helping

them to know the next steps and to understand exactly what they will be doing without feeling overwhelmed or pressured.

Continue to implement these four steps into your sales process and you will see improvements in your efforts. Along with these steps there are other tactics that you can implement into your efforts to see even better results. Asking the right questions is one of those tactics.

Correctly Using Questions

Do you often feel frustrated when you talk with people about your business, but never see any results come from it? As frustrating as this can be, oftentimes the problem is the way we present ourselves and our company. About three years ago, I was working with a business builder that was feeling quite discouraged about their business. I decided that I would tag along with them over a period of a few days to listen to what they were doing and how it was being received. They knew all of the correct information about the company, they were passionate in their delivery—you could really see they loved their company—but they did not ask a single question! After listening to this for a few days, I decided to ask what they knew about their prospects from talking with them—sadly they couldn't answer that question. They had gotten to know nothing about the people they were talking with, they did not know what their needs were, or how they could help them with the products and services they were offering.

When we do all of the talking and don't ask questions, we set the standard for a one-size-fits-all approach—and this just does not work. Shift your focus slightly and talk much less. Get your prospect, customer, or business builder talking and sharing their story with you. Questions allow us to know what their problems and needs are so that we can provide solutions, instead of being a pushy salesperson. Now, I am by no means saying you need to spend your entire conversation asking question after question—you don't want them to feel like they are being interrogated—but you need to be asking a sufficient amount of

116

questions. Asking questions will help you get to know them, what you can do to help them, and the problems they have, so you can give them solid, confident answers.

Depending on the conversation, you need to ask a natural amount of questions that works for the particular situation. Generally, start your conversation out with a question like, "Have you heard of [your company or a certain product or service]?" or "Have you ever used products or services like these before?" Questions like these really get people talking and opening up. They also show how much people know about your company and what you need to share. Imagine going to a restaurant, sitting at a table, and immediately hearing your server start talking about every item on the menu. No one wants to sit and listen to that! Instead they should ask if you have been to the restaurant before, if you have any questions about the menu, or if you have any special requests. The answers to these questions help your server customize what they say to you. This is exactly what we need to be doing—customizing what we say. Once you know more about your prospects and what they know about your company, ask more questions. Based on the answers they give, ask more questions guiding the conversation in a natural direction.

When asking questions, make sure you're not simply asking yes or no questions. Again, the goal is to get them to open up. When people see that you're actively listening and that you care, they are going to talk more and feel much more comfortable. Ask questions that are relevant to what you're talking about and don't make them too personal.

There are hundreds of different questions you could ask, but remember your ultimate goal is to find their pain point. When I say pain point, I simply mean what motivates them to act and to find a way you can help them. Be careful to not make this up. Really find a way your company can benefit them. As you listen and ask the right questions, you will find out what that is. Everyone is at a different place in their life and their needs are going to vary. For some people they may need to make a bit of extra money, for others it might be that they struggle with health issues and could use a product you offer to help them, still others might want to have more time with their family and friends or to simply enjoy life. No matter what their pain point might be, everyone has something that motivates them to change or make things better in their lives.

Take a couple minutes to think about your past interactions. Are you asking sufficient questions? Are you asking the right questions? Do your questions guide the conversation? Now that you have answered these questions, let's do a simple activity to help show the importance of asking questions. Find someone who can help you out and have them play your prospect, customer, or business builder. Your goal is to get to know them. Simply ask a few questions to get to know this person better, find out what's going on in their life, and see how you can help them. Don't think or talk about your company. Remember, the goal of this is to simply get to know this person better and to find a way to help them. You'll do this by only asking questions—no other conversation is needed. Simply ask the right questions and get them talking. If your conversation ends too soon, seems weird, or doesn't flow correctly, you might not be asking the right questions. See the example below:

Question - Hey! How have you been?

Answer - Been great! Life is a bit busy but things are good.

Question - Great to hear that, What's been keeping you so busy? Anything exciting or new?

Answer - I actually started a new job—and things have been crazy with my family, so it's been a bit busy.

Question - Congratulations! What's the new job? Do you love it?

Answer - I work for a company designing software, and I love it!

Question - Busy with a ton of training?

Answer - Yes. Things have been so crazy.

Question - Since you're so busy, could I bring your family dinner one night this week?

This example is basic—and of course, is not going to happen exactly this way in every conversation—but guess what? I figured out what the pain point was from the questions I asked. My friend had started a new job, training was hectic, and they did not have a ton of extra time, so I offered dinner to provide a solution to give them a bit more time. Like I said before, you don't want to ask too many questions, but it is important to ask questions. This activity is simply to get you to ask questions—and to ask the right ones. Now that you have done this, or once you feel comfortable, it's time to present your company to someone by only asking questions. See the example below:

Question - Hey! How are things going?

Answer - Doing ok, thanks.

Question - What's new since the last time we talked?

Answer - Not much. My husband lost his job and that has been a bit tough, but things are good.

Question - Does he have any potential job leads?

Answer - He has been applying for jobs, but nothing yet. Hard times.

Question - Would you mind if I made a quick suggestion that might help?

Answer - Sure!

Question - Have you ever thought about owning your own business?

Answer - No, but that could be nice.

Question - Could we set up a time to talk next week? I have a business opportunity that might help you make a bit of extra money on the side and could potentially turn into something much bigger if you want it to.

Answer - Sounds great! Let's do it.

Again, a conversation might not go exactly like this, but it should illustrate the logical flow of conversation and how you can get to know them and help guide them to see the need for your company. By taking time to practice, understand, and use questions correctly, you will be unstoppable.

> **Tip:** What you say is so important in the sales process. However, have you taken the time to consider that there is even more to a successful interaction other than just the words you have to say? People pay close attention to your body language, the tone of your voice, your eye contact, and more. Each of these forms of communication will either contribute to gaining your prospects' and customers' trust or it will detract from it. It's important for you to be genuine and communicate confidence through these other forms of communication. People can generally tell if you're nervous or unsure of yourself.
>
> Body language can speak volumes about you as a person, how you feel about your company, and speak to your confidence. Based off of your body language, some people may not trust you, they may feel disrespected, they might not take you seriously, etc.

Overcoming Obstacles

Have you heard things like this before? *I love it, but can't afford it. I need to go home and talk to my spouse. I get paid a week from Friday and would love to get started then. Not sure this is something I could do.* I am constantly asked how to overcome obstacles or objections and how to get past the doubts or concerns people have. Truthfully, it's simple. As you get to know the person and ask the right questions, you're going to be surprised how natural it is for you to answer their concerns. However, at times concerns will still come up and there are a few things you can do to counteract them. These include:

- **Assume the Yes** - Oftentimes we give people a way out or an exit plan before they even tell us they are not interested. When talking with someone, talk as if they are going to say yes. Avoid saying things that can create doubts in their minds like, "I know it's expensive", or "It may not be something that interests you". Saying things like this make them question what you're going to say and doubt your credibility.

- **Adding Value** - If they are questioning the things you're saying, you're probably not giving them sufficient value. Help them to really see the impact your company can have in their life—when they really understand the value, they will not be able to imagine their life without what your company offers.

- **Ask Situational Questions** - Ask questions that pertain to their current situation and find ways to make connections between their situation and your products or services. Asking questions about their situation will reveal potential areas where you can offer the value spoken about before. This will help when prospects present excuses or concerns about why they can't or shouldn't move forward with purchasing. Oftentimes people do have the money, but it's getting them to think about it in a situation that hits close to home and a product or service that can really help them.

Invitation to Act vs The Close

Oftentimes you hear people talk about the close and the importance of it. People will take it as far as saying, "If you don't try to close every conversation then you're not a success." The close is absolutely one of the most important parts of the sales process. However, it's not necessary in every conversation. Those that strive to make a close happen in every conversation often come off as pushy, inconsiderate, and only out for their own gain—ultimately they are not nearly as successful as they could be. Now before you think I am crazy, let me explain why I say this and help you see why tweaking this strategy a bit will generate much more success.

The close is just like it sounds—it's the end of a conversation, the action of purchasing your product or service, and moving forward as a customer and/or business builder. A successful close gets your prospect making the decision on their own to see why it's needed and to get them to act. Let me say it another way, the close is absolutely important and necessary in order to get your prospects to purchase.

When closing, it's important to remember the following items:

- **Be Confident** - So many times we freak out when we get to the point of closing—we start to question ourselves, doubt the price, become nervous, or create doubts for our prospects as well. Let them know you're confident that their decision is the correct one, and that you're there to help them every step of the way. Also, it's important to be confident with their decisions. So if they decide to purchase a certain item or go with a certain starter package, you be confident in their decision with them. Hear them out and let them know that you support their choice.

- **Simple and Smooth** - The close needs to be kept simple and smooth. They need to know exactly what they need to do to make a purchase, get started, or become a business builder. Be careful not to overcomplicate it or overwhelm them by using words they might not know. So much of their experience will be based upon the closing process and how simple it might be.

- **Short and Direct** - Keep your close short and direct. When the time is correct to close the deal, keep it about the close and don't go into everything else. Let them know what's needed and be direct with them. Oftentimes people talk and talk during this part. Just let them know exactly what they need and let it go from there.

- **Act Now** - If the close happens naturally—like it should—then they should be acting at that very moment. Don't give them an opportunity to do it later, come back to it, or postpone. It's important to get them acting at that very moment.

- **Control** - During the close, it's important to be assertive and stay in control of the process to get them started. Don't have them sign up on their own—do it with them. Be there to work with them, help them, and get the job done.

Every time you talk with someone you're taking them on a journey. You're asking them questions, getting them to open up, and guiding them to the end goal. The end goal will be different for each person. For some, they may become customers, others may become business builders, and sometimes they simply want to learn more and later find out it's not for them. Based on the idea that every person is different—having different goals or being at different places in our lives—does it not make sense that we should have a different strategy for each of these people as we work with them?

Instead of focusing on a close, your new goal should include an invitation to act in every interaction you have. This simply means inviting or committing them to do something more. For some people this may be as simple as inviting them to learn more, attend one of your classes, to participate in a phone call, to have a follow up chat, or to purchase something from you. Again, every conversation you have is going to be different and it's important to customize your invitation to meet their individual needs. As you ask correct questions and listen to what they have to say, you will better know their needs and you will be able to cater your invitation to act to what they need.

The Upsell

So often people talk about upselling someone like it's a bad thing, and let me tell you something, when executed correctly it is one of the best things you can do for your business, and even your customers. The upsell is all about adding on extra items the customer might need, to help them better understand your company, and to better benefit from its products or services. Now, notice I said adding extra items the customer needs, not extra items you think they need, or extra items to boost your volume.

It has been proven multiple times that people like options. Give your customers options and let them see the value and make the decision themselves. If you have a starter package for your company, use the one the company offers as your basic starter package and then try offering different higher valued packages from that point that include additional products or services. Providing your customers with options will allow them to make the best choice for what works for them. You will be surprised that oftentimes they might not go for the cheapest option, but something in the middle. This is a win for them because they are getting extra items to benefit them. It's a win for you because you have been able to upsell items and boost your business more.

Mastering the upsell is a lot easier than you might think. There is no set goal, dollar amount, or number of items you must offer someone—in addition to what they are already purchasing—to be a success. Simply help more people purchase more products. If you can get ten people to purchase an extra ten dollars each month you are growing your business. This all comes down to properly educating them and adding value to their lives, and helping them see the benefits your company offers. If you can help them see the value and need for the extra product, they will purchase and be satisfied and your business will grow.

> **Tip:** When deciding what to work on or what to accomplish during your day, always start with Revenue Generating Activities (RGA's)! RGA's are anything that will increase volume, grow your business, and help you to see immediate results. It's super easy to get caught up in all of the little things that need to be done to grow your business, However, it's absolutely necessary to set aside a bit of time at the beginning of each day, to focus on generating revenue and increasing your volume.
>
> Here are a few ideas to help you know what would be a successful RGA and what might not be top priority:
>
> Successful RGA's
>
> 1. *Calls* - Call customers who have not ordered, share promotions or incentives, get business builders calling their teams, and help them know what they need to say and do.
> 2. *Prospecting* - Talk with new prospects—introduce yourself and

connect with them. Take every opportunity you get to talk with someone and tell them about you, your business, and how it can help them. Connect in person, on social media, over the phone, or wherever—just connect!

Unsuccessful RGA's

1. *Building a Website* - This can be important and a huge asset to your business, but won't increase volume immediately. When focusing a portion of your time on RGA's, make sure to focus on activities that will potentially increase volume immediately.
2. *Education Emails* - This is super important, but again, this is not the time to execute this activity when focusing on RGA's.

Start a portion of each day focusing on RGA's and you will see a noticeable difference in a small amount of time. If you can only do one thing for your business on a busy day, make it an RGA.

Applying the principles in this chapter will make a huge difference in your ability to be a better, more successful salesperson. However, I have come to realize that sales is much more than the things we do, the things we say, or the way we present our companies. We live in a day and age that everything we do is sales. Each and everyone of us have been raised with the mentality of being the best we can be and as we do this we are selling ourselves. We are naturally salespeople—it's a part of who we are as humans and it's something that comes more natural for us than you might think. Everything in this book focuses on sales.

As you develop yourself to become a better person, you will become a better salesperson; as you market your business and your company, you are a salesperson; as you're out talking to people, creating outlines, looking for new people to benefit from your company, you are being a salesperson; as you teach classes and educate your team, you are a salesperson, and as you strive to be the best leader and lead others to be the best version of themselves, you—again—are a salesperson. Everything we do in this business can be tied back to this idea. Stand tall and be proud of what you do, and be prepared to make a difference in the lives of others through your efforts.

To Do List

☐ Accept the fact that you are a salesperson

☐ Commit to being an honest, helpful salesperson

☐ Understand the differences between the close and the invitation to act and apply them to your efforts

☐ Complete three RGA's before you do anything else each time you work your business

☐ Start using the upsell with your customers, business builders, and prospects

 Tip: To learn more, follow me at facebook.com/trainwithjustin

Chapter Notes

Chapter 5
Classes

Why Classes

I remember my very first time teaching a class about my company and it was far from perfect! I showed up to the venue 15 minutes before the class started and I was not completely prepared—and I was super nervous. To my surprise, everyone that confirmed to come actually showed up ready to learn and participate. As exciting and rare as this was, it took my nervousness to an entire new level. I was shaky, sweaty, and my voice was trembling. I remember thinking to myself, "Why am I doing this?! I am not ready." Once it was time to start the class I found at least ten other things I "needed" to do, to postpone starting. Finally, about 15 minutes after the class was supposed to have started, I stood up and started talking.

> **Tip:** If you find yourself getting nervous before a class, find a quiet place and sit down for five minutes. Take a few deep breaths and focus on the end goal. Why are you having these classes? The answer is simple—to grow your business and become a success. Focus on your future success and your breathing and the nerves will ease up.

I spoke super fast, wasn't able to answer basic questions, and couldn't focus on my audience. I simply wasn't doing a good job. The class continued and because I was speaking so fast, we were ahead of schedule. I quickly finished the topic, briefly asked if anyone had questions—secretly had my fingers crossed that they wouldn't—thanked them, ended the class, and ran to hide in the bathroom. I was so happy it was over, but I missed a crucial piece—I did not even invite the participants attending to do anything. Looking back, I did it all wrong. Because of the failures I saw from this class, I was determined to never let this happen again. However, since then I have come to learn exactly what it takes to give a successful class. When done correctly, they can be a huge resource to your business.

Classes are effective tools that contribute to the success of your business. However, I can confidently say that 95% of the time they are not done correctly—just like my first class. This may sound harsh, but take a few minutes and think about the classes you have given. How did they go? Did you find new business builders? Did you find new customers? Did you increase volume? Did you have a good amount of people attend? Sadly, I have talked with so many people in your position and they simply haven't seen the success they had expected to see, leaving them discouraged and frustrated. These frustrations may lead to a lack of improving in this area or even abandoning this valuable tool altogether.

It doesn't have to be this way. I want you to open your mind and follow along with me as I give you a new and different way to teach a class. If you can put these tactics and strategies into practice you will be able to answer all of the previous questions asked with a resounding yes. All of the techniques I will teach you can be used in both online and in-person classes. These techniques will work for everyone because it will equip you with everything you need to create a simple and effective system that will work for you and your unique personality.

Once these techniques have been mastered and you are hosting effective classes, you will experience a new level of success. You will see an increased number of qualified leads—prospects actually interested in what you have to say, and not just saying "yes" to get you off their back—better motivated business builders, and loyal customers.

I remember when it finally came together for me and I gave my first successful class. I saw a drastic increase in volume, people actually wanted to attend, I was asking engaging questions, and I was getting amazing interaction from the audience. This was seriously a game changer. What a stark difference it was from my first class. Instead of running out of the room, I stayed to talk, signed people up, and enjoyed myself. Over the next several sections I will teach you exactly what you need to know to experience this for yourself.

Take a few minutes to think about your past experiences with your classes and what made them successful or unsuccessful. I've included a few aspects of successful and unsuccessful classes below, that could either make or break your efforts.

Successful classes are:

- **Scheduled** - Classes must be planned in advance to give participants enough notice to find time in their schedules to plan to attend.

- **On Time** - Start and end your classes on time. Be respectful of others' schedules.

- **Well-Prepared** - Be prepared and look professional. Don't just make it up as you go.

- **Presented Confidently** - Preparation will build your confidence and being confident will give you the needed credibility for a successful class.

- **Action Driven** - Classes must contain a call to action or an invitation to act—something to take participants to the next step. If this portion of the class is missed the entire class was a waste of time and will not be a success.

- **Presented Passionately** - Be passionate, exciting, and fun to watch and listen to. This is easier when you have educated yourself on and have a personal connection with your company's products or services.

 Reference: Please see the Eduction chapter in this book for more information about the importance of educating yourself.

- **Focused on Value** - Don't focus so much on the sale, focus instead on giving your participants value. Add something of benefit to their lives and they will be glad they attended your class.

- **Interactive** - Keep your audience engaged, ask questions, and get feedback and opinions from the group. Don't be the only one talking the entire time.

- **Hosted at a Presentable Location** - You can teach a class anywhere, but be sure to have things clean and organized. A messy house or venue can be a distraction.

- **Beneficial** - Focus less on what your company's products or services do and more on teaching how to use them, how they will benefit from them, and how to implement these things into their lives.

- **Fun** - Have fun and encourage others to have fun. When people are enjoying themselves and feel comfortable they will be more likely to become loyal clients who purchase regularly.

Unsuccessful classes are:

- **Last Minute** - When classes are planned on the fly they give participants no time to plan to attend.

- **Not On Schedule** - Starting whenever you want, waiting for people to show up, and not ending on time creates frustration and boredom for participants.

> **Tip:** Not being on schedule constantly comes across as being lazy. You don't want to be seen by your customers or business builders as someone who can't be on time or someone that doesn't make their own class a priority.
>
> If you struggle being on time or sticking to a schedule, try setting your clock 20 minutes fast and set reminders for everything. Work on this and be determined to improve. This will make a huge difference in the success of your class and the relationship you have with your business builders and customers.

- **Not Prepared** - Classes that are thrown together last minute, not thought out, and not well put together are less effective than those that are adequately prepared.

- **Lacking a Close or Invite** - Don't assume that participants know how to proceed or move forward. They have been educated and instructed, but have not been given a clear invitation to act. Prospects will likely not act unless you invite them to.

- **Overly Passionate** - Remember, your participants are getting to know you and your company, they don't necessarily share the same passion you have for it yet. Be excited and help them see that, but don't be the crazy person that people can't relate with.

- **Overly Pushy** - Having a clear invitation to act is important. Encouraging participants to purchase and make a decision is also important. However, don't be that annoying, pushy, disrespectful salesperson.

Reference: Please see the Sales Chapter in this book for more information on a successful invitation to act and close.

- **Focused on Sales** - Sales are super important, however, they do not need to be your main focus. Participants need to leave feeling encouraged, motivated, and informed to make a better decision, and not like they were just drilled about buying something or there to just support your family.

- **Silent** - When you dominate the conversation and exclude your audience from participating it will lead to boredom and frustration. Interaction keeps them engaged.

Tip: Remember to pay attention to your audience. You need to have a good idea of how the participants are feeling at all times. Are they engaged? Are they bored? Are they interacting?

- **Cluttered and Messy** - A messy venue or display can cause distractions and make people feel uncomfortable.

> **Tip:** Keep in mind, "clean and organized" doesn't mean it needs to be perfect. Remember your team is watching you, so make sure you're not overly stressing about the perfection of your venue. You want your business builders to leave your class thinking they could duplicate a similar class.

- **Overwhelming** - It can be distracting if you cram all the facts, numbers, and statistics into one class.

- **Boring** - People are taking time out of their life to come and listen to you— don't put them to sleep! Make them glad they chose to attend your class instead of doing something else.

Types of Classes

Before you start planning classes, it's important to understand the different types of classes you can host and how to execute them successfully. Like I mentioned previously, when done correctly, classes can be a huge asset to your business.

There are hundreds of different types of classes you could host. However, I recommend sticking to these five main types and mastering them. As you get into the preparation stages for your class, it's important to keep in mind that these are simply class types and they should be customized to meet the needs of you and your participants. Have fun with it and make them a success.

1. **Business or Opportunity Class Template**

   Goal: Educate and excite about your business opportunity
   Length: 45-75 minutes

This is usually designed to talk about the opportunity part of your business and what it can do for someone's life. These classes would be a great time to discuss making money, a bit about the industry, and any details about the business side of your company—like your compensation plan, bonuses, incentive trips, etc. Keep it simple and lighthearted, but informative.

7:00-7:20 pm

Welcome! I'm so excited you have chosen to join us tonight to talk about an opportunity that has changed the lives of many. Tonight we will have fun, help each other grow closer to achieving our financial goals, and move one step closer to achieving financial freedom.

I would like you to think about three questions tonight as we discuss this opportunity. Take a few minutes to write them down with your answers. We will come back to these questions multiple times throughout the night.

1. What motivates you to achieve financial success?

2. What can you start doing today to change your current financial situation?

3. If you feel excited, motivated, and eager to grow a business with [your company], are you ready to act tonight to get started?

Now that you have answered these three questions, I would like to briefly tell you a bit about myself.

- *Time*: Share how long you have been with your company.

- *Impact*: Explain what your company has done for your life and the lives of those closest to you. Be passionate, but don't be overbearing or too passionate—find the right balance.

I also like to use this time to explain what it costs to get started. This can be done simply by saying, "This is the best $300 dollar investment I have ever made! And because of it, I have seen huge changes in my life."

- *Goals:* Share some of your financial goals, what motivates you to be a success, and help others do the same.

- *Invite:* Invite them to get to know you more at the end of the class. Thank them again for being there and make sure they know you appreciate their time.

7:20-7:50 pm

Now that we have gotten to know each other a bit more, let's dive in and get started.

- *Company History*: Briefly explain how long your company has been around and share your company's income disclosure statement as well as a few fun facts about your company. Don't give out too much detail—just enough to get them the information they need and to get them interested.

> **Tip:** It may not always be appropriate to share your company's income disclosure or to talk about money. However, I will often have it at my classes to use for reference or bring it up when people start talking about income.

- *Compensation Plan*: Highlight a few easy-to-understand areas of the compensation plan. The goal is to help them see the potential without overwhelming them. I like to focus on simple bonuses and quick ways they can make income from the start.

- *Success Stories*: Share a few stories of others who have seen

137

changes in their lives because of your company's opportunity. These stories should excite people and be something they can relate to. Don't just share the stories highlighting only those with the highest income. Most of your participants won't be able to relate with the idea of making a crazy amount of money in a month's time. But they can relate with an individual who wanted to make a couple hundred extra dollars each month to pay off one extra bill, the individual who simply wanted to get out of debt, or a single parent who is simply building the business so they could send their child to college. Most importantly be relatable.

> **Tip:** Keep your story relevant to the group you're meeting with. Whether you're talking with successful business owners, stay-at-home mothers, recent college graduates, retirees, or anyone else, you'll want to relate your story to what would matter and motivate them. Basically consider and know your audience beforehand.

- *Investment:* Remind them what it costs to get started, the time they will need to invest, and what it takes for someone to succeed.

- *Assess Interest:* This might be one of my favorite parts of the class and it's something that will really help you see success. Take a few minutes to ask your participants if they're interested in getting started and making things happen. Some of them will say yes and others will say no or nothing at all—and that's just what we want. The entire point of this step is to prepare those interested for the action items (listed in the next bullet) and allow those that are not interested to feel less pressured because in their minds you will be talking to those that are interested and not them.

- *Action Items:* At this point you should give those interested five to seven action items they could start doing today to grow their business. This will help them get excited and motivated to get to work and also help them to see how simple it can be to get started. Remember, they need to feel like it's something they can do and succeed at. While you have been talking to those who said they are interested (from your interest assessment), the other participants—who were not interested or said nothing—have been listening. The entire time they have been listening without feeling pressured. However, they have heard the same items as those that were interested and can now make a better assessment to see if they could be successful as well. They are now better prepared to join you as a business builder when you do your actual invitation to act. This step is huge! Taking the pressure off of those who did not seem interested initially, will give them time to think about your business and see that it's something they can really do themselves.

Tip: Share the First Steps to the Summit booklet with your new business builders from this class to give them action items they can start with from day one.

7:50-8:00 pm

Wow, what a night we have had! Thanks so much for your participation and for being here. Take a few minutes and look over the three questions I asked at the beginning of the class. Think about what motivates you to be a success, what you can do today to change your financial situation, and if you're feeling excited and eager about what we have discussed. Are you ready to act?

How many of you see the opportunity as something you can use in your life? Together let's move one step closer to our goals by taking the first step in changing our current financial situation!

- *Ask Questions*

- *Resolve Concerns*

- *Invitation to Act*

- *Thank Them and End the Class*

2. **Practical Implementation Class Template**

   Goal: Implementation of your company's products or services
   Length: 60-90 minutes

   Use these classes to show creative ways of implementing your company's products or services into your participants' lives. If you can successfully show someone how to do this, you will have a lifelong customer. These classes can be a lot of fun and a huge help in increasing volume.

   Being creative is important, however, giving simple and practical ways of implementing your company into their daily life and routine is a must. They need to leave this class knowing exactly what to do with the product or service and how to use it in place of other items or services. If they can truly grasp the simplicity of using your company, it will be a success.

   Tip: When preparing for these classes, remember to make it amazing, but keep it simple. Business builders and potential business builders are watching everything you do from the setup, the display, and the presentation. They need to be able to leave feeling like they could duplicate what you did successfully.

   7:00-7:20 pm

   Thanks for coming out tonight. I'm so excited to share with you over the next hour to hour and a half, how to use [your products or services] and how to incorporate them into your life.

One thing I have come to realize since using [your products or services] is that there are unlimited ways to incorporate [your company] into our daily lives and routines. The great thing is, when done correctly, we can save money, learn about new ideas, and truly live a better and happier life.

Take a couple minutes to think about these few questions:

1. What are you most excited to learn about tonight?

2. What is one item you could incorporate into your life from tonight's class?

3. Are you open to living a better life starting today?

7:20-8:00 pm

My main goal tonight is to help you see how simple it will be to incorporate [your company] into your daily lives and the benefits of doing so. I would like to briefly tell you a bit about myself and help you understand my story and why I started with [your company].

- *Time:* Share how long you have used your company's product or service and what got you started.

- *Impact:* Explain what your company has done for you and those closest to you. Share how your company's products or services have impacted you for the better and what made you stop using other company's similar products or services.

- *Goals:* Share some of your personal goals with your company's products or services and help them see why you're so passionate about sharing these products or services with others.

- *Invite:* Invite them to get to know more about your story at the end of the class. Thank them for attending and make sure they know you're appreciative of their time.

Before we get started tonight, I would like to ask you to open your minds to new ideas and be open to the possibility of what [your company] can really do for you. Be prepared to learn a lot of new things that will change your life.

Now that we have gotten to know each other, let's get started.

- *Company Info:* Share a bit about your company and what makes them great.

- *Introduce Products or Services:* Explain what they are, what they do, and the benefit of each. Give two to five examples of common and simple ways to implement these into daily life. Remember to keep it simple. They need to know they can implement them without having more stress in their life. When possible, show them how to make something, or a clear way to really put this into action.

- *Hands-on Time:* Allow for an opportunity to see, touch, and really relate with your company's product or service. If you have a product, get it in their hands. Let them touch it, feel it, smell it, etc. If your company offers a service, show them the impact and difference this service makes.

- *Bring it Back:* Now that they have been taught and experienced what you have to offer, remind them how to implement your company in their life and how they will benefit from doing so. Help them see how simple it really is and that it's 100% worth it.

8:00-8:30 pm

I hope you all enjoyed learning more about [your products or services] and that you've been able to see how simple it can be to implement these into your life. I remember when I got started, it was a bit overwhelming, but things changed once I was able to understand how simple the switch could be.

- *Ask Questions*

- *Resolve Concerns*

- *Invitation to Act*

- *Thank Them and End the Class*

3. **Reward Yourself Template**

   Goal: Reward your VIP customers and business builders
   Length: 1-6 hours (time for these classes may vary)

   This is a newer class topic for me, but it has been a huge success. This could be used for your VIP customers or business builders. This is something to reward them for being great, for contributing to your business, and for making a difference. Reward them and help them feel appreciated while continuing to educate and teach them.

   Welcome! We are here because of you and the great things you have accomplished (or for being loyal, if they are a customer). Today is designed to reward you for your dedication and loyalty. Let's have fun, enjoy each other's company, and celebrate *you*!

   - *Rewards:* Have a way to recognize these people. Not everyone needs recognition, simply pick three to five of the top individuals and recognize them.

> **Tip:** Take some time before the class and think about those attending. Identify what they have done since the last class, how they have been involved in the business, or how many times they have consistently purchased as a customer. Keep a list of those you have recognized and make sure you try to recognize everyone over time in these classes.

- *Activity:* Have some sort of activity to motivate, encourage, and thank them. This could be a dinner, a spa treatment, a day at the pool, or something fun. Remember to start small—this does not need to be huge.

 Tip: Include these activities in the budget portion of your Marketing Plan. Remember, you can make someone feel special without spending a penny.

- *Special Announcement:* Give them special information before others hear about it. This could be in the form of new products, team promotions, or anything to help them feel special and like an insider. If you're able to give them an opportunity to purchase something before others, this is the time to do so. If meeting with business builders, this is a great time to have a planning session to help them feel supported. Overall, the goal is to make them feel special and appreciated.

- *Ask Questions*

- *Resolve Concerns*

- *Invitation to Act*

- *Thank Them and End the Class*

4. **Luncheon or Coffee Hour Template**

Goal: Short and casual class designed to educate on a set topic
Length: 30-60 minutes

These are the simplest classes and can be done in less than an hour. Meet a group of people for lunch or grab a quick drink and educate. Take this time to teach and instruct while enjoying a casual, no-pressure atmosphere.

- *Welcome:* This type of class does not need an official welcome. Coffee or lunch classes need to be kept super short and casual. If you have never met the person, keep it simple and introduce yourself. If you're meeting with someone you know, say "hello", make small talk, and move on.

- *Educate and Inform:* Usually you meet up to discuss a particular topic. After you have said hello, dive directly in and discuss the topic at hand. Keep it simple, precise, and low key.

Tip: These classes should be planned, and are oftentimes more successful when treated as a follow-up from a previous conversation or appointment.

- *Ask Questions*

- *Resolve Concerns*

- *Invitation to Act*

- *Thank Them and End the Class*

5. **Intro Class Template**

Goal: Introduce your company
Duration: 60-90 minutes

This is more of a typical class, which teaches them about your company's products or services, helps them get to know more about what the company can do for them. This does not always have to be the same topic. It could be an intro to a different part of the company, a different product, and so on. Don't be afraid to get creative.

7:00-7:20 pm

Thanks for coming out tonight! I am excited to talk with you over the next hour or so about something that has become super important to me in my life.

How many of you have heard about [your company]? Let me tell you something—[how ever long ago you started] years ago I had never heard of them either.

- *Your Story:* Explain how you came in contact with the company and what has made it important to you in your life.

- *Company History:* Discuss how long your company has been around, what makes them different, how it has helped others, and what makes you so passionate about it.

- *Fun Facts:* Ask questions to get them to relate with your company's products or services. If you're with a health company this could be a health question, if you're with a financial company it could be about interest or savings, and so on. Get creative with these questions and make them fun and engaging.

As we get started tonight I would love for you to write down one thing: *What do you want to take away from our time together tonight?* Think about this throughout the night.

7:20-8:00 pm

Tonight we are going to be talking about... (If your company has a starter kit, talk about that. If there are a few services you prefer, talk about those—just pick something. Your goal is to give an introduction to your company and this can be done by explaining any of your company's products or services.)

Tip: When teaching introductory classes, you should never worry about running out of content or teaching the same class over and over. Use different products or services offered by your company and then teach about the same product or service, but to a different market. For example, New Moms and [your product or service], Students and [your product or service], Business Owners and [your product or service], and so on. You should never feel like you don't know what to say or what to teach.

- *What's the Catch?:* Many times people get concerned and worried because they know you are going to try to sell them something. Handle this at the very beginning. Let them know the price and that by the end of the night, you're confident they will see the value in what you have to offer. This allows your participants to focus on what you're teaching and not worrying about what you're going to try to get them to purchase.

- *Introduce:* Take time to introduce the products, and go into some depth about what they do. This is the time to give them all of the basic information and help them understand the impact your company can have in their life. You would want to give less information than you would in your practical implementation class, but enough to help them get excited and see how simple it can be to be involved with your company.

- *Questions:* Make sure you have sufficient time for questions. It's important that they really get to interact with you in this class more than any of the others. They need to ask questions, get answers, and feel good about what you're saying.

8:00-8:30 pm

Thanks so much for coming out tonight! It has been a great night and I hope you have all enjoyed yourselves.

- *Ask Questions*

- *Resolve Concerns*

- *Invitation to Act*

- *Thank Them and End the Class*

 Tip: The suggestions above are simply templates to help you with your classes. Make sure you're asking questions to get them involved and excited throughout all parts of the class.

Reference: Please see the Sales chapter in this book for more information on the invitation to act.

How Do I Prepare?

The success of the class starts with the preparation. It is important to create classes that are informative, worth people's time, and something that adds value to their lives. The great thing about preparation is that you will be able to use your content more than once and it will be easier to create future content. You will find tactics listed below that you must do in preparation for a successful class:

1. **Select a Date and Time** - This is a pretty simple task. Set a date far enough out to give yourself time to prepare, time for others to plan to be there, and to provide at least two weeks to market your class. I have noticed Tuesday, Thursday, and Saturday mornings or evenings work best for classes. However, experiment with other days and see what works best for you in your area. Remember that people are typically busy during the week, so keep your classes short.

> **Tip:** Survey your business builders and customers to ask them what days and times work best for them. Getting their input will help avoid excuses when people say they can't make it.

2. **Location** - Pick a location that works for your audience. Also research the location to understand interest and find fun things people like to do in the area—then incorporate these into your classes when possible. Before you select a location, think about your current business builders and customers in a selected geographical area. The more people you have in the area, the easier it will be to get people to attend and to have a successful class.

3. **Topic** - No matter the type of class you will be hosting, it's important to select a topic. What exactly will you be discussing? What product or service will you be covering? Pick a topic that's relevant for your audience and one that is of interest to them. It's important that your topic be engaging, exciting, and something that will help your participants connect with you and your company.

> **Tip:** If you're just getting started it is ok for you to pick topics that you are comfortable with. Start small and once you become better educated or more comfortable with other topics then branch out.

4. **Themes** - Once you have selected a topic, have some fun and pick a theme. These can be anything and should be unique, different, and interesting. Remember to keep it simple so others on your team can visualize themselves doing the same class while having fun. Try doing a Mexican-themed luncheon at a local Mexican restaurant, a casino-themed, reward-yourself class, and so on. Have fun with it. Your theme is the way to make your classes something that everyone wants to be involved with. Picking a theme is an added benefit, but not necessary to have a successful class.

5. **Presentation** - This is the actual physical presentation that you will give and naturally one of the most important parts of your class. It will need to be thought out and prepared. I will show you how to do this in more detail later on in this chapter.

> **Tip:** Once you have prepared your class, take time to practice it. Get in front of the mirror, some friends, or family and practice. Time yourself while doing it to make sure you have the correct amount of content. Get feedback from your friends and family and keep improving your class.

6. **Marketing** - This is key to generating interest and excitement as well as getting people to your class. Take time to think through the details of your class and set up a successful marketing campaign to get people to attend. Here are some of the things you need to do to help market a successful class:

   - *Identify People to Help* - Select three to five business builders within a close geographical proximity to the class. These will be the ones that help you invite people and coordinate things. If you don't have business builders, that's ok. Reach out to friends, family, or anyone you know in the area and ask them if they would be willing to do you a favor and invite people they know to your class.

> **Tip:** When you feel frustrated and can't find someone to help you, ask others for a "favor". People are going to be much more willing to help when you ask them to do a favor for you than if you were to ask them to invite someone to one of your classes. The wording here makes a huge difference. Don't believe me? Give it a try!

   - *Encourage Business Builders to Extend Invitations* - Have your three to five people invite 20 people each. Don't use a

Facebook Event for this, but have them personally connect with 20 people and invite them. Instead send a quick phone call, text message, or something to connect more genuinely with these people.

- *Invite Customers* - Reach out to all of your customers within the geographical area and let them know you're having a class and would love to see them. This is a great opportunity to connect with the customer, answer any questions they might have, and remind them you're there for them if they need something. Again, personally connect with them and don't simply send an invite on Facebook.

Tip: When appropriate, ask customers to come and share their story. This is a great way to get them involved, have an extra testimonial for your participants, and to get the customer to attend the class.

Tip: Incentivize your customers to invite their friends and family! This does not have to be anything huge or crazy, simply let them know they will be entered into a raffle for every three people they invite, or for every five who show up they will receive a nice little gift. Be creative with this, but remember, getting your customers to bring their friends to a class that they are passionate about is huge—and it will give you new potential prospects.

- *Extend Personal Invitations* - Now that you have your business builders and customers inviting people, remember to do your part. Personally invite as many people as possible within the geographical location of your class. I like to have a small flier with me at all times and every person I come in contact with I will give them a copy of the flier for the class. If you don't know a ton of people in the area, take some time, if possible, to walk around and approach local businesses and let them know about it. Have fun and invite people. Classes without people will not be a success.

> **Tip:** Become a walking billboard for your classes! You should be proud of the work you have put in so far, excited to share your passion with others, and should tell everyone about it. Talk with everyone, help them to see your excitement, and get them to attend.

- *Utilize Facebook to Extend Reach* - Use Facebook as a resource to invite people. It should not replace the personal invitations discussed previously. However, it is a great way to promote your classes and extend the reach of your previous efforts.

  ▷ Advertisement Posts: Advertise your class on your Facebook business page as well as your customer and business groups with a simple post. Do this at least twice a week for two weeks prior to the class. You'll want to grab their attention, create excitement to attend, or provide something that will motivate them. Consider using an engaging, appropriate image relating to the class.

> **Tip:** These advertisement posts are in addition to your current scheduled post on your Facebook Groups and Page.

  ▷ Facebook Event: Facebook events are a great way to invite people to your class. It also helps remind your participants of the class and motivates them to attend. Personally invite at least 30 people (in addition to the people you invited in-person), and ask your business builders to invite at least 20 people each. I open this up to all of my business builders, so they can invite individuals they might know in the area. Use your business builder groups to get them involved and inviting people. It is important to be consistent. I like to do two posts a week up until the time of the class. This will keep your class top of mind and create excitement and eagerness to attend.

7. **Incentivize** - Think of incentives and ways to motivate people to attend, show up on time, and to purchase. Incentives can be affordable and yet very motivational for people without breaking the bank. Increase the incentives as you grow your business. People love and will respond to even little incentives.

Reference: Please see the Marketing chapter in this book for more information on the difference between promotions and incentives.

8. **Reminders** - Now that you have invited and incentivized people to attend, don't forget to remind them about the class. Life gets busy and a simple reminder can make a huge difference in the success of your classes.

I know the steps listed above can seem to be a bit complicated and overwhelming, but don't stress. This is the ideal situation and the perfect way of inviting people to attend your classes. Incorporate what parts of it you can and as you grow, apply more and more over time. More than anything, just remember these three things: share your class, promote it, and talk to everyone to drive excitement. If you do these as you're getting started, you will see success.

How Do I Teach? What Do I Teach?

Being a good presenter is imperative to the success of your class. Take time to study this section and make sure you're doing the things to become the best presenter you can be and that you're able to capture and engage your audience. I have found focusing on these areas makes a huge difference:

- **Asking the Right Questions** - I have noticed most people can only focus on what you're saying for approximately seven to ten minutes before something else grabs their attention. By asking questions regularly throughout the class, you can engage your participants more and keep them focused on the material. Getting participants to say "yes" or to agree with what you're saying by using simple questions, will open them up to listen more intently and better retain the information that is presented. This will help them make personal connections to the material and show that you care about them. So ask questions frequently during your class and make sure they are clear and easily understood.

One of my biggest pet peeves is when someone asks a question and then the audience just looks lost or confused (you will notice they look to the ground, start looking around, or ask for clarification). These types of questions can have a negative impact on your class. So it is important to ask the right questions. Take time to think about what you're going to ask, even map them out before your class to make sure you're asking questions frequently to keep your audience engaged. If you can't think of questions that apply, ask them questions like, "Does that make sense?", "Can I give you a simple idea?", or "Would you like to understand more?" Getting your participants to answer questions and be involved will change the success of your class.

> **Reference:** Please see the Sales chapter in this book for specific ideas about what questions to ask.

- **Explaining Things Clearly** - Just because something makes sense to you does not mean it will make sense to someone else. We need to use clear explanations that everyone can understand, but be careful not to insult their intelligence. Before I present, I always try to understand my audience—who will be there, what takeaways they'll want from the class, what their skill level is, and how I can help them to receive value. Once I ponder on these things, I make sure my content and presentation are clear and easily understood. Remember

154

how some things might have been overwhelming or maybe you did not understand all the ins and outs of your company when you first started. These people are in the same spot. Help them understand, teach them, and do so in a way so they can make clear connections between their lives and the material being taught.

- **Encouraging Engagement** - Questions are just one form of engagement. In addition to questions, I like to have different hands-on examples to show them what we are talking about and to discuss how to implement the company in their life. If you're talking about products, pass them out, let them see them, smell them, taste them, and so on. If you're discussing business opportunities, help them to set goals, work with groups to create business plans, or just give them simple ways to get them engaged in your class.

- **Expectations** - Be clear with your expectations. If you're promoting a product or service and you want to try to sell it, that's ok—just be open about it. Share the price, what they'll get, and the details at the beginning of the class. The great thing about doing this, is you get any weirdness out of the way from the beginning. They won't be sitting there thinking—what's the catch, the cost, or what are you trying to sell or promote? That way they'll be able to focus on what you're saying. Also let them know that you want them to interact, be engaged, and ready to learn. Let them know your goals of the class and what you hope they take away from it. Finally, find out their expectations of what they hope to gain from it.

- **Atmosphere** - Create an open and comfortable atmosphere—a place where they feel eager and excited to learn. Doing this will help the entire flow of your class, which will result in a better, overall success. Avoid having a weird, quiet atmosphere that no one wants to be part of. Get people talking, interacting, and working with others from the very beginning.

> **Tip:** Create a fun and comfortable atmosphere before the class starts. Make sure to be set up and ready to go, so ten minutes before the class starts you can be out talking with people, introducing yourself, and getting to know them.

Now that we have identified a few things that will make you a better presenter, let's talk about what you need to do to create content. It's important to follow the steps previously mentioned, but let's be honest, people are coming to your class because of what you are going to talk about. Having well prepared and easy-to-understand content is key to the success of your class.

- **Identify and Understand Your Audience** - As mentioned before, understanding your audience is important to be effective with your class. Take time to complete a needs audit to really understand your audience. Are they there to learn about making money, to use your product or service, or just for fun? Think about how you can help them make connections between the product or service and their lives. Think about what they like, what their pastimes might be, and other interests they may have. Understanding your audience makes a huge difference in the overall success of the class. It will allow you to add value to their lives, which will increase the likelihood that they will buy your product or service. In turn, this will increase volume and result in a better paycheck for you. One thing to keep in mind is that we each have a pain point, something that makes us act. For some people this could be the need to make more money, to have better health for their children, more freedom of time, or resolve a serious life situation that makes your product or service a need to them. As you understand your audience you will be able to speak to these circumstances and really add the needed value. See the example below:

Example:

Pain Points or Needs -

1. Tired of living an unhealthy life.

2. No solutions - They need answers.

3. Need extra money.

4. Wanting to drop a few pounds.

5. Not sure they know enough people to be successful.

*   **Talking Points** - Once you have identified your audience and understand what their needs and pain points are, write down three to seven items you plan to discuss during your class that will address those needs. It's very easy to get off track when you're starting out or to feel nervous about presenting. You might find yourself talking about things that are not important, not sticking to the class schedule, or even rushing through your class. Writing down talking points will not only help you stay on track, but it will help you create the content needed for a successful class. See the example below:

Example:

Pain Point - Tired of living an unhealthy life

Talking Points -

1. Why they are unhealthy.

2. Using (your product or service) can help with stress.

3. Opportunities like mine have the potential to give freedom of time.

4. Three action items that will help them have a healthier life.

5. We offer the solution to their problem—I can't wait to help them.

- **Free Write** - Once you've written these pain points down, start free writing. Set a timer for three to five minutes and write down everything that comes to your mind about the set topic. Don't worry about grammar, wording, or anything other than constantly writing. After you have done this, repeat this activity for all of your talking points. Really get creative here, have fun with this, and write all of the details your audience would need to hear in your class. This will help you create content that will be motivating to your participants and guide them to making the decision to do business with you. See the example below:

Example:

Pain Points or Needs - Tired of living an unhealthy life

Talking Points -

1. Why they are unhealthy.

2. Using (your product or service) can help with stress.

3. Opportunities like mine have the potential to give freedom of time.

4. Three action items that will help them have a healthier life.

5. We offer the solution to their problem—I can't wait to help them.

Free Write -

1. Our company provides solutions to help people become more healthy and happy. We also have a survey that will help them recognize their problems and help them see changes they need to make. I need to help them see the changes and help them want to make them.

2. The following products or services can help them: (List out

products or services that can help them with stress and specific needs.)

3. I could share stories from some of the leaders in the company who enjoy freedom of their time and benefit from having less stress. Show them some fun, practical examples that could help them be excited.

4. I could create a three-step plan to help them get to a happier life. Maybe have it start with educating yourself, followed by applying that education—and afterwards, maybe they could tweak or make changes to improve the results.

5. I need to remind them that we really do have the solution to the problem they have. Sometimes they may not even know they have an issue. However, we can help them see the issue through the solution.

- **Creating a Class Outline** - Now that you have done the free writing and have expounded upon your talking points, let's outline your class. When creating the outline, take time to make sure the class flows well and can be easily understood. Be sure to identify the topics you want to discuss and be prepared. This is the time to really expound upon your talking points. This is the content that you will use to give in your class. See the example below:

Example:

Class Outline

- Welcome - (Use the points from your free write to develop three points you would discuss in your welcome.)

    1. _____

    2. _____

    3. _____

- Questions - (Give one to three questions to get your participants thinking. Use your free write to guide your questions.)

  1. _____

  2. _____

  3. _____

- My Story - (Use your free write to create three solid points about your story with your company.)

  1. _____

  2. _____

  3. _____

- Main Message - (This is the time to be detailed and educate. Expound upon your free write to educate your participants.)

  1. _____

  2. _____

  3. _____

- Ask Questions

- Resolve Concerns

- Invitation to Act - Create two to four invitations and write them out based off of your participants' pain points and your talking points.

- Thank Them and End the Class

Tip: Does your content capture someone or get their attention? This is an absolute must!!! Your content needs to be created with your audience in mind—and be sure to get their attention by drawing them into the topic you're discussing.

Class Length

The length of a class is just as important to its success as the preparation, the content, and the invitation to act. Depending upon the content of your class, the length of time it takes can vary quite a bit. Remember not to make something longer than it needs to be—simple and precise is best. No matter how long it ends up being scheduled for, remember to start and end your class on time. This is often forgotten, but is so important. People live very busy lives and they are taking time to be at your class. Be respectful and professional about their time and thank them for being there.

If you give them an agenda, then stick to it. Participants stop paying attention and get frustrated when things are not on schedule. It also makes a successful invitation to act next to impossible.

Also, don't go overboard. If a class can be short, keep it short. Remember, just because you have a history, passion, or love for your company these participants are new and are still learning. Don't be over the top—keep it simple, basic, and real.

Follow Up

One of the biggest mistakes people make while presenting a class usually doesn't even happen during the class time. They teach an amazing class, capture their participants' attention and interest, and even collect contact information. So what's the mistake? They forget to follow up! This cannot happen if you want good results from your class. The follow up is a crucial part of teaching classes and you'll want it to happen naturally.

Review and implement these few steps when following up:

1. **Collect Contact Information** - Gather appropriate information to follow up with the participants. Getting their name, email, and phone number is the basic information I require to attend a class. Have them check in and register at the beginning of the class for their name badge. This is an easy way of getting all of their contact information. Don't misuse or abuse their information, instead use it to follow up and work with them in the future.

> **Tip:** If you're not comfortable having a registration or you're presenting a class with a group and a registration is not natural for your class, then have a giveaway! Get your participants to fill out the back of a raffle ticket, which will give you all of the information you need for a successful follow up.

2. **Email List** - Having an email list is a simple way to communicate with participants from your class and if you only send one email a month, it shouldn't become an annoyance. These emails are to simply inform them of upcoming classes. Follow the structure below for a simple, successful email:

   - **Greeting** - Simply say hello, wish them well, and give them something to capture their attention. You want them to read the entire email and not just the first few sentences, so make sure you begin with something captivating.

   - **Brief Message** - Take a paragraph or two to share a brief message. This is your opportunity to educate, but keep it simple and short. This is not a full-on education email, but a basic way to briefly educate and help them better understand your company.

   - **Upcoming Classes** - Inform them about classes that you have coming up, explain a bit about each one, and why they should attend. This is your opportunity to get them excited about your future classes and capture their attention. Provide them with the details needed so they can make a decision to attend.

- **Invitation** - Like everything else we do, you need to invite them to act. This could be an invitation to a future class, a way to invite them to apply what you just taught them, or to simply learn more. These invitations need to be simple, clear, and easy to follow.

- **Thank Them and Close** - Thank them for taking their time to learn more about you and your business. Remind them that you are there for them if they need anything and wish them well.

Example:

Hey,

I hope you're doing well. We have some amazing things going on over the next month and I can't wait to share them with you.

As you know, we are committed to providing you with all of the most up-to-date information and I am so excited to tell you a bit more about this [product or service] *(Come up with three to five points about a product or service, your company, or something— just enough to keep what you do fresh in their minds)*.

This month we have quite a bit going on. Check out the schedule below:

- *(List out the dates, times, locations, and topics for your classes.)*

I am so excited for these classes and can't wait to see you there. Which class interests you most? Do you think you could make it out? Please let me know if you're able to attend and I will be sure to reserve you a spot.

I hope you have a great week and if you have any questions

please don't hesitate to let me know!

[Your name]

3. **Common Connecting Point** - When possible, find a way to connect with each person and get to know something personal about them or something that sets them apart. This will be harder as your classes get larger, but you can use your class as the connecting point. Take notes when possible to remember these people and what it was that makes them different. This makes a huge difference when you follow up and it helps them feel like you remember who they are and that they are special.

4. **Two Week Follow Up** - Within two weeks from attending, send them an email, give them a call, or send a simple text thanking them for attending, and to remind them of their invitation. Remember to let them know if they need anything you are there to help them and that they will be receiving emails from you monthly keeping them updated with what's going on. When possible use your common connecting point to make this portion of the follow up a bit more personal.

Facebook Classes

Now that we have discussed in-person classes, I want to discuss an option that is a bit more modern and has the potential to really help you grow an international business. I'm talking about hosting classes using Facebook. Facebook has become an effective business tool that allows you to reach groups and individuals far beyond your geographical location. Whether you're familiar with hosting classes on Facebook or not, you can easily become an expert by following the suggestions listed in this section.

First, take some time to schedule several Facebook classes over the next few months. I teach at least one of these a month, and once they are scheduled, make sure you stick to it. After a few classes you will start to see great success. When hosting a Facebook class, look at it like a lead generation system. The goal is not to sign someone up or increase volume immediately, but to generate a following, create leads, and add value to their life. Facebook is a great platform to use for online classes, so let's dive into the details.

> ⚙ **Tip:** When selecting dates, be sure to keep in mind the holidays or other important dates. It's important to not host your Facebook classes on holiday weekends, but also planning your theme around the holiday could be a great benefit for you.

The first thing you'll want to do is decide where you're going to host your Facebook class—and I don't mean the physical location. Many people set up a "Facebook Event" to host their class. This is one way to do it, however, it is not the most successful option. Participants will not be able to view the page after the event is over, so this only gives you a limited time to capitalize on your content. You've got to think about the bigger picture. You want to not only create a successful class, but also to establish a learning community that participants can return to for future classes that you might offer.

It is because of these reasons that I would suggest setting up a "Facebook Group" to capitalize on your audience. A Facebook Group can be used as your learning academy—a place where people can go to reference any content or materials and keep updated about all classes. In the beginning this may take more work, but in the long run this will be much more successful. This group will be used to host all of your online classes, to gather leads, and to provide a common meeting place for new adds and long time group members to review your previous classes and prepare for new ones.

Here are a few steps to consider when creating your group:

1. **Create your group** - When creating your group, make sure it is public.

2. **Name it** - Give it a simple, but catchy name—something they can recognize as your personal brand and clearly know what will be happening in the group.

3. **Add header image** - Add a header image that shows something fun and relatable to your company and the group theme. This image should be on your personal brand.

4. **Describe it** - Add a simple and clear description. Let group members know you will be hosting regular monthly classes in this group and give them a way to contact you with questions. Encourage them to invite other people to attend these classes as well.

5. **Post in group** - The goal of this group is to educate and get people excited about what your company has to offer. Two weeks before your class, posts should be all about the class, things to look forward to, exciting incentives or promotions, or anything to get them excited about attending the event. During your class you will use this group to post your class content. When classes end, this group is not to replace your other groups or pages and should only be posted in once a week to stay current. The main focus of this group is to be used for classes.

6. **Purpose of class** - The goal of this class is to create leads and generate prospects. As you generate leads your team will grow.

Now that you have created your group, it is time to market your class. This can be a fun way to promote your class topics and generate some excitement for them. The key to successful marketing efforts comes down to preparation and creativity. To help with this, I've listed some steps below to follow that will effectively market your class:

1. Create a Facebook Event from your personal Facebook profile and not from your group, and add in all the details of the class. Remember to let them know that the class will take place in

166

your Facebook Group and that you will be adding them to the group once they RSVP. They need to know that the class will be held online and that they will have to be on their phone or on a computer to participate.

> **Tip:** Let your participants know that they don't have to be glued to the computer or their phone the entire time and they can be free to come and go as they wish. This is a benefit of these Facebook classes—they can work them in around their schedules. You will be surprised how many people actually think they need to be watching the entire time without interruption, so make sure to communicate this.

2. Just like an in-person class, you will need to select a time that works for everyone and choose a type of class and a theme of interest. The more interest you have, the more success the class will be. When selecting the time duration of your class, be sure to provide enough days to cover all the content you want covered. Classes should be at least one day long, but generally not more than three days. This will give participants time to access your posts, read through them, and interact with them. Also help them to not feel pressured or rushed.

> **Tip:** I like to host my classes on a Friday evening and then have them run all day Saturday. People love the idea of attending a class from their homes and having something fun to do over the weekend.

3. Take time to personally invite 60-100 people to each online class by sending them a simple Facebook invite. Find people that you think will be interested in and excited about the topic and theme of your class. Don't just invite everyone because you want a large group, but take time to really invite those that will be interested in your set topic.

> **Tip:** Remember, it is ok to invite your existing customers and business builders to these classes. Find those that are interested and would benefit and invite them to the class. Naturally, after each class you will be starting a new one and inviting new interested people, so the participants in the group from previous classes will be able to see and learn from the content as well.

4. Ask your team, both business builders and customers, to invite anyone to the class. Assign set business builders to invite 30-50 people each and let them know the benefits of inviting them will add huge success to their business. Simply let customers know you have the class going on and if they know anyone that might be interested to invite them.

> **Tip:** You can even give your customers a small incentive to invite their friends. Also take time to get your business builders involved. Ask them to make a video, share a story, be on the group to answer questions, and so on. Giving them an assignment will help them be more active and involved.

5. Remember to add everyone who says they are attending or are interested in attending on your Facebook Event to your Facebook Group. It is important they are in the group to participate in the class and to avoid missing out on anything going on. Add people to your group on a regular basis.

> **Tip:** You can post a link to your public group on your Facebook Event invite and make it a bit easier for people to join the group on their own.

6. Because the class is not being held on the event page, it is important to post on this page before the class. Post two times

a week to promote and get people excited about the event. Remember, this is to simply remind them of the class and to generate excitement.

Now that we have created the group and marketed the class, it's time to talk about creating the content and flow of your class. Creating the content is the most important part of an online class. Once it is created, you can recycle it in the future, allow your teams to use it, or utilize it for other efforts.

1. **Welcome** - Just like in your in-person class, it is important to have a solid welcome to create a fun atmosphere to get participants excited. I also like to introduce myself in this portion of the class, explain a little about my story, and share something interesting about me. I then want to get to know something interesting about the participants. The welcome section should be broken into three to five posts.

2. **Educate and Add Value** - The education section, like any other class, needs to be the most important part of your class. This will take up the bulk of your class and depending on its length, it should have at least ten posts with a maximum of 35 posts. This is based off of a Friday evening and an all-day Saturday class. If your class is three days, you will add content. Be creative with your content and help them see the value. The most important part of this section is to add value and to give your participants something to think about—a way for them to implement your product or service into their life. The goal here is not to sell, but to educate.

3. **Interacting** - This step should go hand in hand with education. It should get them involved through teaching and educating. With an online class this can be a bit tricky, but very important. Ask them to share an experience, or get them to relate with what you're talking about. Create a video of you using your product or service. Remember to be creative to get them involved.

4. **Invitation** - Like anything else you do there must be an invitation to act. Invite your participants to try a product or service, implement something into their lives, attend a future class, or something similar. Make it simple and clear.

> **Tip:** Invitation to act posts shouldn't only be found at the end of your class. It is important to have them throughout the class. You can invite people to take advantage of promotions, try a product, or even promote your company's starter package. Be smart when you use these posts and make sure to not overuse them.

5. **Promote** - Simply promote future classes and get them excited to attend.

6. **Thank Them and Close** - End the class by reminding them that there will be future classes in the group and remember to thank them for their time. The benefit of hosting classes in this group is they have access to the content all the time and are already in your group for future classes. Let them know you're here to help them and to answer any questions they may have.

> **Tip:** Be sure to pin a post at the top of your group with links to each post. You can do this by clicking on the drop down arrow in the top right corner of your post and selecting "pin". This makes it very simple for future participants to read your content in order. Also it makes it easier to find previous class content since it will be all in one post.

Example:
February 22, 2015 Intro Class

Post 1 - Post Link
Post 2 - Post Link
Post 3 - Post Link

Post 4 - Post Link

All posts should be linked and included in this main post. After the class, simply unpin the post.

 Tip: Here is the schedule and outline of a typical Facebook Class that I've used.

Friday 6:00-9:00 pm:
6:00   Welcome! Excited to be with you.
6:15   A bit about me.
6:30   Tell me a bit about you.
6:45   Class expectations.
7:00   Education and interaction (Educate, involve, and get them learning how to implement your company into their life).
7:30   Education and interaction.
8:00   Education and interaction.
8:15   Promote (This is a great time to let them know about your special offers on promotion for this class or anything else).
8:30   Education and interaction.
8:45   Questions.
9:00   Have a great night! Excited for tomorrow.

Saturday 9:00am-9:00pm:
9:00   Welcome back.
9:30   What was your favorite part from yesterday?
10:00-2:00 (Post every 30 minutes) Education and interaction.
3:00   Promote.
4:00-7:00 (Post every hour) Education and interaction.
8:00   Promote.
8:15   Questions.
8:30   Who's ready to try some of these amazing products or services?
8:45   Promote (Use this to promote upcoming classes in the group).
9:00   Thanks for participating! What's stopping you from getting started?

Now that we have discussed the flow of your class and have talked about the details, let's discuss important items to consider while creating your content. Unlike an in-person class, you won't be interacting face-to-face with your participants, so you need to make sure your content grabs their attention and keeps them engaged.

- **Images** - Never do a post without an image of some sort. I would rather see you post a bad image than nothing at all. Take time to find images from your company, images of hobbies and things you like, or images that relate to the themes of your class. Posts without images will most likely not be read and are guaranteed not to have much interaction. Take the extra time to find engaging pictures that will grab their attention. You don't need to have a fancy graphic for each one or something specifically designed, but a picture is necessary. Make sure your images are good quality (not blurry), bright, and attention-grabbing, as they scroll through their newsfeed.

- **Written Text** - Facebook posts should be kept short, to the point, and fun. People literally have hundreds of posts in their newsfeed and your posts need to stand out from the rest of them. If your post is long, most likely someone will just read the first sentence or so and then move on—if they read anything at all. You want and need them reading everything you type, so keep it concise. Be real with your content and capture your voice or personality with each post. You want your participants to get to know you from your content, so be sure to be you and have fun with it.

- **Facebook Live and Videos** - Facebook Live posts are an amazing way to welcome people to your class, to teach them, and to help them relate with you. I like to use live videos to welcome people to my classes, invite them to act, and to thank them at the end of the class. These can also be used to educate your participants. Personally, I prefer using videos to educate because the content can be saved and used for future classes and given to downlines. When hosting a Facebook Live event or doing a video, remember to look professional, have good lighting, and get started right from the beginning. Don't sit around waiting for people to join to build an audience. Most of your views will be replays, so don't waste people's time. Dive into your topic and get started as soon as you turn the camera on. Both Facebook Lives and videos are a great way to connect with people in your group.

> **Tip:** Keep track of people who have been interacting, showing interest, or seem to be paying attention to what you have to say. These participants should become your main focus—connect with them, work with them, and be there to support them. Don't overwhelm them or send them a lot of messages, just simply keep in contact with them and make sure you help them if they are ready to move forward. Sometimes I like to invite these people to a phone call or to meet up to talk more in depth about the class. Do this when it feels appropriate and natural.

Remember, classes can be a huge game changer in your business. Review this section anytime you teach a class and master the principles taught here. There are a lot of ideas discussed in this chapter and they can seem overwhelming. Give yourself some time, set goals, and before you know it you will have mastered the concepts in this chapter.

To Do List

☐ Take a few minutes to evaluate your classes and make sure you are following the points for a successful class

☐ Schedule your next four classes

☐ Identify which class types you want to try

☐ Start to prepare for your first class

☐ Create a regular email to send out about your classes

☐ Schedule your first Facebook class

Tip: To learn more, follow me at facebook.com/trainwithjustin

Chapter Notes

Chapter 6
Education

Have you ever heard someone talk about a product or service and thought to yourself "they just get it"? I know I have. How do you think they got to that point? Over time, I have come to find out that it wasn't because they were inherently better, they just had spent time educating themselves on the topic. It is so important once you commit to becoming a success, that you educate yourself on the ins and outs of your company and really learn what it is that will make you a success.

You don't have to know everything, nor do you need to wait to build a business until you have educated yourself. Dive in now and get started, but always be open to learning new things. You can become that person who "gets it", but to do that it is important that you educate yourself in the following areas:

- **Company Products or Services:** Constantly learn about what your company provides and personally use their products or services. Learn how they work and what benefits they offer. These experiences will help you become familiar with those products or services, and in turn your credibility will become genuine and effective.

   It makes it much more complicated to promote a product or service that you don't understand or use yourself. Utilize information provided by your company, the Internet, your uplines, crosslines, and team members to constantly learn more. Also take some time to learn a bit about your competitors. What are some of the things they do differently? What makes you use the company you do?

- **Business and Marketing:** Educate yourself on basic business practices and how to be a successful business owner within the industry. As you learn new ideas and concepts put them into practice. Marketing and business concepts are constantly changing. Continually apply the principles in this book to help you stay current as trends change.

> **Reference:** Please see the Marketing chapter in this book to help you with your marketing needs.

- **Self Development:** Continue developing your strengths, learn new skills and attributes, and work hard at becoming the best you can be. As you improve your knowledge and skill set, you will create a positive atmosphere regarding education. This will help motivate your team members to do the same.

> **Tip:** Constantly strive to be growing and learning. Situations and circumstances change and you should too. As you do this it will help you tackle new challenges and opportunities as they arise.

> **Reference:** Please see the Self Development and Leadership chapters in this book for more information on becoming a better version of you.

Teach Others

Now that we have discussed a bit about your personal education and how it is important to develop yourself, it's time to start educating your organization. This will consist of both your business builders and customers. But before we get into the details, let's define what each of those are:

Business Builders are members of your organization that not only use the company's products or services, but are actively selling, promoting, and growing their team. There isn't a specific personality required for a business builder, which is one of the reasons why it's important to talk to everyone about your business. You never know who might be interested in business building.

Customers are members of your organization who purchase and use your company's products or services. They show loyalty to you and your company. However, they typically are not interested in building the business, promoting the company, or making money off of it. Keep this in mind as you support them. Don't push the business if they want to just be customers. An organization with more customers than business builders is a successful organization.

> **Tip:** Keep business builders and customers separate and don't pressure the customers or make them feel like they need to be building a business to be involved in the company. However, all of your customers should know that there is an opportunity available for them if they ever decide to become interested. And as soon as they express interest they then become a business builder and should be supported as such.

Now that you know the difference between business builders and customers, it is crucial to create solid systems and provide ways to continually educate the members of your organization. This will help your business builders become more effective in their efforts and your customers will continue to purchase the products or services you offer. Let's dive in!

Business Builders

When people join your team and are excited to grow a successful business, it is important to keep that excitement and motivation alive. One way to do that is to continually educate them on what your company offers. They need to have information about the company, the compensation plans, tips and tricks, and details regarding the products and services. Of course there are many ways to do this, but I have found that a few simple tools have made it easier for me to support and educate my team. I support my business builders using the following tools:

1. Facebook Business Groups

2. Email Campaigns

3. Weekly Business Calls

1. Facebook Business Groups

Using Facebook business groups is an effective way to support and educate your business builders on the details of their business. I have split my business builders into two groups—new business builders and advanced business builders. Separating these two groups allows me to provide more targeted content to these audiences. It's like the milk before meat concept—you wouldn't give a baby steak before it had teeth to chew it. It's the same with your new business builders. They'll need to know the basics and have a solid foundation before they start using more advanced practices. Remember, you want to set them up to succeed.

New Business Builders

This group is designed to teach, educate, and help them understand the basics of what they need to do to become a success. It includes a 60-day Prospecting Plan (included in the Prospecting chapter of this book), education on details regarding the business side of the company, tips and tricks to be a success, and much more.

It is important to publish at least two posts a day and one post on the weekend days in this group, to provide the necessary support your new business builders need. Remember, this is your opportunity to connect and build relationships. Make sure to be active and involved—respond to comments, questions, and concerns.

> **Tip:** As your team grows, ask leaders to help you post and take on some of the workload from this group.

Ensure that your team feels that they can be open in this group to make comments and ask questions—and that their questions will be well received. If you want to see interaction in this group, you will need to be involved and an active participant. You can also use it to share promotions, incentives, and anything extra to make it fun and exciting. If they feel as though they are a part of the team and that they can succeed, they will stick around and together you will be much more successful.

To help in these efforts, I want to give you a practical template of how to organize your posts. Below, you'll find what a typical week should look like in this group. I like to stick to these topics weekly and have fun with them. If you use these and follow the guidelines for what each post needs, you will be educating your team and you will see success.

Monday

Post 1: Tips for Success - Many times in the industry, new business builders struggle knowing what to do, how to succeed, and how to use their time for the best reward. This post should be a simple quick tip—something to help them know what to do, or how to take the next step. Keep it short, fun, and be creative.

Invite them to give feedback letting you know how the tips went for them, what they did well, and what they struggled with. The invitation is just as important as the tip. It creates an atmosphere of support and trust and is essential as you build a team of strong, independent leaders.

Example Posts:

1. Set a goal to talk to at least five new prospects this week about our amazing company. Don't be nervous! Let us know how it goes.

2. Take a minute and call your newest team member, welcome them to the team, and let them know you're here to help them. If you've already welcomed them, move on to someone else on your team, or check in on them again. Help them feel welcomed!

Post 2: Promotions and Incentives - This is used to motivate your team and bring awareness to any company or team promotions or incentives that are going on for the week or month. Use this post to teach about the promotions and incentives being offered. Creating value will spark interest and generate volume.

Example Posts:

1. Take advantage this month with 15% off this great item! Have you had the opportunity to try it before? If not, what are you waiting for?

2. Did you know [promotional item] can be used to [do this] and to [do this]? This is one of my all-time favorites and something I use daily! Be sure to check it out and let me know if you have any questions.

> **Tip:** Remember, even if they don't purchase, they will have information to teach others—which is the goal of this group.

Tuesday

Post 1: First 60 Days - The first 60 days are the most important for both business builders and customers. This post should be all about helping your new business builders use the 60-day Prospecting Plan to see results within the first two months. Teach about this program, help them see how simple it can be, and share results or success stories of those who have used it. Remember, your advanced leaders will also be in this group so have them share their stories from using this program. If a business builder can see success within the first 60 days, they will be more likely to stick around and help you grow your business.

Example Posts:

1. Welcome! Let's make your first 60 days count! What are you doing daily to make your business dreams become a reality?

2. Have you made your daily contacts? During your first 60 days it is important to connect with as many people as possible. Remember when connecting, keep it simple, add value to their lives, and find out something unique about them. Give them something to remember you by. Generating leads will guarantee your success. Welcome to the team!!!

3. Congratulations Amy! Amy has been working the business for 12 days and has personally found two new customers. Remember to keep working hard and you will see your dreams become a reality. We are here to help you if you need anything.

Post 2: Business Goals - This post is designed to set and share goals with your new business builders as well as to rely on the team to keep them accountable. Also use this to teach about the importance of goals, goal setting, and how to make their goals a reality. I love showing these new business builders examples of people who have made their goals happen, even the little goals that we all have. Keep your goals simple and specific.

Example Posts:

1. Please share your monthly goals—new members, volume, classes held, etc. Let us know what you plan on doing this month so we can better help you.

2. Take time to set goals, post them in a place you can see them regularly, and work hard. Have a great month and let's make those goals a reality!

3. Wow! I am so happy for Samantha. She set a goal to find ten new customers this month and not only did she meet her goal, but she signed up 12 new customers! Thanks for your dedication Samantha—great job! Have you reached your goals this month?

Wednesday

Post 1: Company Difference - Have fun with this post and help your new business builders see the reasons they joined your company. Share what makes your company different, special, and unique. You can even use this as an opportunity to share about the team and what makes your team different. All companies have something good to offer and something that makes them unique. Share these unique differences because they will come up multiple times as they talk with their prospects.

Example Post:

1. Did you know [your company] has one of the most generous compensation plans in the industry? Not only do we have amazing products, but our opportunity truly changes people's lives.

Post 2: Motivational Thoughts - Simply find a motivational quote or video that will encourage people to become better. Don't overthink this—just keep it simple, uplifting, and fun.

Example Post:

1. "Stay focused, work hard, and just do it!"

Thursday

Post 1: Ranks - Use this post to teach about your company's ranks, requirements to achieve these ranks, and what reward they will receive when they do. This post needs to be interesting, but also direct. Use your company's income disclosure if you're going to give dollar amounts for the ranks so that it's accurate and not exaggerated.

Example Posts:

1. It takes on average three hours per week for six months to hit the rank of [enter rank]. Can you do it faster? [Attach a copy of your income disclosure with this post]

2. In order to reach the rank of [specific rank] you need to have a regular monthly volume of [amount].

Post 2: Tips for Success - Follow the same steps previously described under Monday.

Friday

Post 1: Compensation Plan - This post should teach about your compensation plan. Pick a small portion of the plan and explain it. Remember to break these down into small, digestible portions because these plans can be quite overwhelming for new business builders. Talk about terminology, volume, bonuses, payouts, etc.

Example Post:

1. Let's talk about [your company bonus] bonus. Did you know that when you sign someone up, you make [dollar amount]? What a generous company we work with!

Post 2: Team Spotlight - Pick someone on your team and recognize them for something. This does not need to be something huge or anything crazy, but people need reinforcement and love to be recognized—and if they know you do this on a regular basis they will work to receive this recognition. I like to recognize team members for their first sign up, the most sign ups in a given period, positive leaders, the biggest increase in volume, and so on. Really, you can recognize them for anything!

Example Posts:

1. Congratulations [team member's name]! What an amazing job this week signing up ten new customers!!!

2. Thanks [team member's name]! We could not have pulled off a successful event this week without your help! #rockstar

Saturday

Post 1: Revenue Generating Activities - Give them ideas of activities they could do to generate revenue and what they can do to see an immediate increase in volume.

Example Posts:

1. Take ten minutes today and call five of your customers who have not placed an order and see how they are doing. Get to know them and see if there is anything you can do to help them.

2. Try to generate volume daily. Send out two to three "thank you" or "thinking of you" messages or cards. Send them something special to let them know you're thinking of them.

3. Hit the streets and talk with everyone! Add five new prospects to your potential list. Talk with anyone and everyone you see, make a connection, and share what you do. This can be a bit scary, but have fun with it and really get to know people.

Sunday

Post 1: Motivational Thoughts - Follow the same steps previously described under Wednesday.

 Tip: Along with the suggested material for each post, add an engaging photo to enhance the text and to grab their attention.

Advanced Business Builders

This group is for my more advanced business builders. Once they have hit a certain rank or volume, I add them to this group. You can decide at what point this is, but for me it is around the second rank or after doing a couple thousand dollars in volume. I want them to have had some experience with enrolling new members, learning about the company, and having a good idea of what they are doing before they come into this group.

This group is used to train and educate as well, but more than that it is designed to help people strategize, set goals for rank advancement, and focus on taking their business to the next level. This is a great place to create trust and utilize each other's strengths to generate new ideas. Be open, real, and honest with your team.

Be sure they know that this is a private group and items discussed will stay within the team. This is also the "money maker" group and should be treated that way. These people will be the ones making you money and you will be helping them make money. Support them and help them stretch themselves to be successful.

This is my absolute favorite group! This group allows you to see success and grow closer as a team. Unlike the previous business group—which had themed posts for each day of the week—this group has posts for each day of the month. I've broken down each day and described what type of content should be posted. Here is what a typical month should look like:

Day 1: *Monthly Goals* - Set specific detailed goals with your team. These goals should be focused around individual growth, team focus, and meaningful tasks to help your business builders progress.

Example Posts:

1. Have you thought about your monthly goals? What will you do to increase volume? Beat last month's volume and make this your best month yet!

2. This month's goal will be education. Set a reminder to learn something new each day and teach something new to your business builders or customers.

Day 2: *Leadership Spotlight* - This is a great post to recognize new rank advancements, overachievers, and great leaders. Really make your leaders feel special and appreciated. You can combine multiple spotlight's in one post. See example below:

Example Post:

1. Congratulations to [team member], [team member], [team member], and [team member] for hitting [rank title]! Great job!

    Congratulations [team member's name], for signing up the most people last month. She found ten new customers—way to go! Congratulations [team member's name], for going above and beyond with your customer service! You have created lifetime, loyal customers.

> **Tip:** Usually you can come up with something to recognize people with. However, at times it might be difficult to do that, so use this post to educate on a leadership quality or on a leader you admire. I have even made creative comments that get people laughing and recognize them for random things like, "Way to go Sally, you officially survived the month! Sally is one amazing, committed person and kept going when the month got hard! We appreciate you!!!" Have fun with it and remember to add value.

Day 3: *Promotions and Incentives* - Let your team know about promotions and incentives your team or company may have. Also use this post to really incentivize them to make the month great and successful.

Example Posts:

1. Dinner is on me!!! If you find over ten new customers this month, I'll treat you to a delicious meal!

2. Wow! I am shocked by the promotions this month. (Share a graphic or something from your company reminding them what the promotion is. If your company does not have a graphic, be sure to expound on the details of the promotion.)

3. Be sure to teach your team about these great promotions! What an amazing opportunity to help others save money and grow your business.

Day 4: *How to Build Leaders* - Just because your builders are a bit more advanced in their business, it does not mean they understand how to build others into leaders. Share with them steps on how to be the best leader they can be and teach others how to become leaders.

Example Posts:

1. Do your business builders and customers feel comfortable working with you? Are you there to help and support them?

2. Did you know that most leaders start out as customers? Help your customers feel supported and informed.

3. Take some time this week to do some personal development. What leadership qualities do you need to better develop?

 Reference: Please see the Leadership chapter in this book for more information on becoming a better leader.

Day 5: *Contest Announcement* - Always have some type of contest for your advanced business builders. This does not have to be something crazy or something that will break the bank, but it should be something fun and challenging to help them grow their business. The goal of these posts are to educate, so have them participate in a contest and always use the interaction to educate and teach.

Example Posts:

1. Take a picture of you putting the company into action. Show us how you use your product or service and be entered in for a chance to win a $15 gift certificate.

2. Take a tip from this group and teach it! Record yourself doing so

and post the video in the comments below. The winner will be selected to receive an amazing prize basket.

Day 6: *Motivational Thought* - Give a simple, clear, and motivating thought. You can find a favorite quote or a nice video to use.

Example Post:

1. "To be a champ, you have to believe in yourself when nobody else will." - Sugar Ray Robinson

Day 7: *Tips and Tricks* - Give your leaders simple tips, tricks, and ideas to have a successful month. Think of what has worked for you in the past or ask other teammates or leaders in your company what works for them. Sometimes we get so caught up in working on things, we forget that simple suggestions can go a long way. This is one of my favorite posts and has impacted my business in huge ways.

Example Post:

1. Struggling to find new prospects? Not sure how to talk to new people? Remember, the secret is just doing it. Start meeting new people, get to know someone at a child's sporting event, introduce yourself to an employee at the grocery store, or get to know someone that seems to be having a hard day.

   Really listen and get to know them. When the time is right, they to will listen to you. Your goal is not to sell, but to build relationships—the sale will come later.

Day 8: *Maximizing the Compensation Plan* - Understanding the compensation plan is great! However, really knowing how to maximize it and understand the strategy behind it is so important as a leader. Share ways that your team can maximize and understand the strategy behind your compensation plan. If you don't know how to do this, it's ok to ask others or to do more personal research.

Example Posts:

1. Did you know that [specific bonus] can make you [dollar amount] extra money each month? So many of us forget to qualify for this! What could you do with an extra [dollar amount] monthly?

2. You can receive commissions on [number] levels down from you! Remember to focus on all individuals interested in building the business. Help them grow and support them with what they need to succeed, no matter where they are in your organization.

Day 9: *Sales Training* - Provide your leaders with different ways or angles to present your company's products or services. Help them generate new ideas for sales and make it seem natural. So many times people get caught up in having the perfect presentation when they just need to start—help them get started.

Example Posts:

1. *Listen* - Really listen to what the prospect has to say. Get to know them and genuinely take interest in them, their interests, and life.

2. *Understand* - Really try to understand what the prospect is saying and where they are coming from.

3. *Relate* - Find a way to relate with your prospect. Talk to them about their interests and find common ground you can talk about. If you can't find common ground personally, then think of someone you know and relate with them.

4. *Connect* - Always find a way to connect with others. It will help you be more genuine and they will remember you and be comfortable talking and working with you.

5. *Present* - When conversations flow naturally and your prospects can see you care, they will ask what your interests are and what you do. Take the opportunity to share with them about your business. Add value, tell them about you as a person, and connect that with your passion for your business.

6. *Invite* - Never forget to extend invitations. This may be a casual invite, or something more structured depending on the conversation—but an invitation is a must. It could be as simple as a follow up call the next week to discuss more details, or as big as purchasing product at that moment. Remember to keep it natural.

Day 10: *Education on Promotions* - Teach your team about the promotions, help them understand what they are and how to use them. This will help them be able to teach their customers and business builders about these benefits.

Example Post:

1. This month [product or service] is on promotion! Did you know it can be used to [benefit], and [benefit]? This is an amazing promotion and one that needs to be shared with your team! Educate them on the benefits of this great promotion.

Day 11: *Leader vs. Boss* - Identify characteristics that differ between a leader and boss and teach them about these differences.

Example Post:

1. How do you lead? Are you motivating your team with fear, consequences, or alternatives? Or do you lead with kindness, support, and assurance? Do they know they can count on you to help them grow? Being a leader is key to success within the industry.

Day 12: *Prospecting Tips* - This is another one of my favorite posts and a great opportunity to give new ideas or suggestions to improve finding new prospects. Share ideas with your builders, ask them for tips that they have found successful, and learn together.

Example Posts:

1. Who have you talked to today? Take time and talk to everyone—

even the postman! Remember, the key to prospecting is talking to everyone.

2. When talking to new prospects, remember to quickly find a way to connect. Share something that sets you apart from others and identify a way to remember them and they will remember you!

Reference: Please see the Prospecting chapter in this book for more tips on successful prospecting.

Day 13: *Motivational Thought* - Follow the same steps as previously described under Day 6.

Day 14: *Tips and Tricks* - Follow the same steps as previously described under Day 7.

Day 15: *Halfway Mark!* - This is simply what it seems. Remind your team that they are halfway done with the month, remind them of their goals, and help them set tactics to make things happen.

Example Posts:

1. Congratulations! We made it halfway through the month! You all are killing it this month! Remember your goals and let's make the second half of the month just as good as the first.

2. Have you looked at your goals recently? We have hit the halfway mark, let's finish strong and make it count! Let me know how I can help.

Day 16: *What Motivates You* - Share what inspires you to be a success and to be involved in the business. Have your leaders do the same. Ask questions that get them sharing and talking about their inspirations.

Example Posts:

1. What an amazing story of motivation! [name of leader], a top leader in our company, has just recently started a program to help give back to [his/her] local community. We work in an industry with limitless opportunities! How will you help and inspire others?

2. Today I had the opportunity to sit down with one of my leaders and celebrate the success they are having. We are changing lives in our company, and it is an amazing feeling to be a part of that! Thanks for all the hard work each of you do to help change the lives of others.

Day 17: *Social Media* - Give a few quick tips or tricks on how to engage others on social media. Keep it simple and don't overcomplicate it.

Example Post:

1. Remember to be real and be yourself in every Facebook post. Add value to the reader's life and share something engaging, interesting, or educational so they stop and read your post instead of scrolling on.

Day 18: *RGA's* - Give suggestions of revenue-generating activities that can be done on a daily basis to help increase volume.

Example Posts:

1. Try contacting two to three of your customers that have not ordered within the last six weeks. Talk with them, see how you can help them, and update them on any promotions or new products. Remember to invite them to place an order.

2. Contact five of your friends and family on Facebook and send them a brief message. Let them know you are looking to grow your business and ask them if they know anyone that might be

interested. This is a great way to open the door and not put any pressure on friends or family!

Day 19: *Passion = Success* - Show your passion, help your team show theirs, and be sure to share it.

> **Tip:** Being passionate is contagious. As you show your passion, it will positively affect your team members and snowball from there.

Example Posts:

1. What makes you passionate? How do you share that passion with others?

2. Passion is contagious! Seeing others get excited when they start their journey makes it all worth it! What makes it worth it for you?

Day 20: *Motivational Thought* - Follow the same steps as previously described under Day 6.

Day 21: *Tips and Tricks* - Follow the same steps as previously described under Day 7.

Day 22: *Strengths and Weaknesses* - Help your business builders identify their strengths and weaknesses and then set plans to improve them. Identifying strengths and weaknesses will help your team be more successful. Work together to make improvements when needed.

Example Post:

1. What are your top five strengths and weaknesses? How are you making your weaknesses into strengths?

Day 23: *Classes* - Give simple tips and tricks to having a successful class. Share both good and bad experiences you have had and what you have learned from them.

Example Posts:

1. Remember to start and end your classes on time. Showing respect for others' schedules goes a long way!

2. Have a clean, presentable setup. Being organized and having a clean setup helps your participants to be able to focus on what you're saying and not on the setup behind you. Keep it simple, clean, and inviting.

 Reference: Please see the Classes chapter in this book for more ideas on hosting a successful class.

Day 24: *Service* - Use this post to discuss service opportunities, to help others, and to give back. Share examples of what you do and what others are doing to give back. A team that serves together will become more united.

Example Posts:

1. Take some time to give back and help those in need. Getting out once a week in the local community can make a huge difference for you and your business.

2. One of the great things I love about the industry is the ability to give back! Take advantage of opportunities to give back!

Day 25: *Commission Reveal* - This is my absolute favorite post. Share your commission check amount and have others do it as well. This builds trust amongst the team, and really helps people get excited and motivated to build a successful business.

Example Post:

1. It's time to post your commissions! Remember, this post stays within the group and is not intended to brag, but simply to show what hard work and dedication can do! Keep up the good work and be proud of your progress.

> ⊛ **Tip:** I understand this might be uncomfortable for some people. However, being real and honest with your team will have such a huge impact on your business. Don't be afraid to make yourself vulnerable—it will help you grow with your team. Remind your team that these amounts shared are not to boast, but to simply show improvement and what can be possible with hard work and dedication. Also remind them that these posts are not to be shared and they are to stay within the group.

Day 26: *5 Days Left* - Focus on how great the month has been and give them a simple reminder that there are only five days left to make it a great month.

Example Post:

1. Five days to go! What a great month it has been. Keep going and finish strong. We are here if you need anything!

Day 27: *Motivational Thought* - Follow the same steps as previously described under Day 6.

Day 28: *Tips and Tricks* - Follow the same steps as previously described under Day 7.

Day 29: *Rank Advancement* - Who's going to hit their goals this month? Who will be ranking up? Be there to help them with anything they need at the end of the month so they can hit their goals.

Examples Posts:

1. Who is going to rank up this month? What can I do to help you make it happen?

2. [Name of team member] is so close to hitting the rank of [rank]! Keep going, you can do this—we are here to help if you need anything!

Day 30: *Finish Strong* - Remind your team members to finish strong and not to give up on the last day. So much can happen in one day! Work hard as a team and give that final push to make things happen—you will be so glad you did.

Example Post:

1. We are in the final few hours of the month—push hard, stay focused, and make your goals a reality! Keep up the good work.

2. Email Campaigns

Email campaigns are a great way to keep your team informed and excited about the business. I use this as an opportunity to educate more in depth on set topics than I would be able to do in the Facebook Groups. This gives your business builders one more avenue to educate themselves and provides something they can reference when needed.

Email campaigns are different than a newsletter in the sense that they are organized to go out in a specific order and not to simply advertise what's going on within a current time period. You should have approximately 12 emails and they should go out about once per week. Emails should be around five paragraphs in length at the most and should teach about a set topic. These emails should commence as soon as someone starts the business and will provide a constant form of education as the new business builders embark on this great journey.

Let's break down the basic structure of each email. Make sure to add these to every business email you send out. They need to include the following steps:

Basic Email Structure

- **Greeting** - Start with a simple hello and a nice welcome. Thank them for their time and remember to keep it short. This does not need to be a huge section in the email, but is quite important to have. You want to capture their attention within the first sentence or two so they continue reading the emails to get to the good stuff.

- **Last Week Follow Up** - Follow up on the previous week's email by asking a few questions, or by talking about what you discussed. Say something like, "I hope you enjoyed trying [product/service]."

- **Education** - This section should be the bulk of the email. Take some time (a paragraph or two) to educate them about a new topic and its benefits. Teach them how to use or apply it in their life.

- **Invitation** - Invite them to use and apply something you just taught them about. This could be an invitation to apply the newly taught principle, or to research and learn more about it.

- **Motivation** - Now that you have taught and invited them to do something new, show them you believe in them. Your business builders will be more successful knowing they have you in their corner supporting them.

- **Farewell** - Close the email, thank them for their time, and leave them excited and ready for next week's communication.

Now that you have seen how each email should be structured, you'll find a list of topics and examples for your email campaign below:

Email 1: *Welcome to the Team* - Keep this email fun, simple, and upbeat. This is your first interaction with the business builder, so you will want to make them feel like they belong to something bigger. Give them a bit of information about you and other leaders on the team. Basically let them know you are there to support and guide them through the journey of their new business.

Example:

Welcome!

I'm so excited to have you as a member of our team and I'm glad you've made the decision to take advantage of this amazing opportunity—to create a successful business, which will change your life forever. Over the next several weeks we will be sending you an email once a week, which will explain the details of the business, provide tips and tricks to becoming a success, and everything you need to know to change your life and create a solid, successful business.

Now that you have made the decision to create a business, it's time to get started. Take some time this week and get to know the business, the products or services, the compensation plan, and then immerse yourself as much as you can into all of these things. There is quite a bit to learn and it can feel a bit overwhelming at times, so take it in sections and remember that you will learn as you go.

This week take some time to set some goals—specific things you would like to see happen and then get organized. Let us know what we can do to help—even if you need help setting your goals.

Remember, this is the beginning of an amazing opportunity, something that will change your life. We are a team and are here to help you along the way to be a success, so reach out if you need anything.

Have a great week! We are excited to work with you!

[Your team name or your name]

> **Tip:** Some of your new business builders may have been customers for years, and that's ok. Remember to treat them like they are a brand new business builder and start them from the beginning.

Email 2: *What to Do - My First Month* - Give them step-by-step instructions of what they should be doing in their first month. Help them plan set activities and train them on efforts that will produce results. Share with them different sections from this book and help them be a success.

Example:

Hello!

I hope you had a great first week getting to know a bit more about the company and this amazing business opportunity. How did your goal-setting go? Did you set goals that will challenge you, but also be realistic? We would love to see your goals. Please share them with us on the business Facebook Group.

This week we are going to talk about a few things to do during your first month to help you get started so you will succeed.

- Remember to have your goals in a place where you can see them regularly. A goal in sight is one that will be accomplished. Remember to look at them often, focus on them, and be prepared to make them happen.

- Create a list of people that might be interested. You will oftentimes hear people advise others to create a list of everyone they know—this is a decent idea. However, it is important to talk with those first that you think would be interested and willing to listen. Identify if they will be a customer or a business builder. If you're not sure, label them as a customer.

- Reach out to at least five people a week from your list. Tell them about what you're doing, get to know them a bit more, and really listen to them. The goal is not to be super eager and crazy about what you're doing, but to strengthen your connection and have a prepared way to add value to their life. If they say no, don't be upset, just mark it on your list. Who knows, they might come around in time. Sometimes timing is the biggest determining factor whether or not someone is ready to be a customer or business builder.

- Continue learning and take time to learn new things daily. Read these emails, use the Facebook Groups, and learn about the company and what the business has to offer.

Get ready to make this week great, and be sure to take some time to start implementing these things. Remember to set goals, work on your list, and start talking to people. Start this week by doing these things and you will see results soon. Remember, this business opportunity has the potential to change your life and the lives of others.

If you need anything, we are here! We're so excited to have you on the team.

Have a great week,

[Your team name or your name]

Email 3: *What Motivates You to Succeed?* - Help them understand what drives you to be a success and identify what will help them succeed and be motivated. Staying motivated within the first two months is super important to the longevity of your business builder.

Example:

Hello!

I hope you are having another great week and that you enjoyed your second week as a business builder. How are things going for you? How did you feel contacting the people on your list and what did they say? No matter what may have happened, don't get discouraged. Remember, everyone does things according to their own timing.

As we start week three, focus more on motivation and what makes you motivated to become a success. One of the things we teach all business builders in the industry is to identify their "why" and what it is exactly that motivates them to succeed. Have you thought about this? Is it helping others? Taking care of your family? Traveling the world? Whatever it may be, hold on to it, stay focused by what it is that motivates you, and when times get tough remember your "why" and it will keep you going.

One of my passions is helping others succeed. The industry allows us the opportunity to help others make their dreams become a reality. Take some time this week and define your "why", know what it is that motivates you, and find ways to start living it now. If you're comfortable, please share your "why" with us on the Facebook Group. We are excited to get to know you more.

Have a great week! Can't wait to see your "why" and for you to experience great success.

[Your team name or your name]

Email 4: *Company Difference* - Share a few facts about your company and what makes them special. Help them understand why their choice to start their own business was the correct one. Every company has something that makes them stand apart and be a bit different—focus on these.

Example:

Hey!

I hope this email finds you well. How does it feel having defined your "why"? Knowing exactly what motivates you to be a success and what drives you to work when times get tough can be so helpful and motivating. I remember the first time I defined my "why" and at that point I felt like I was unstoppable and was ready to succeed! Hold onto this excitement and stay focused and you will do well.

This week I want to talk a bit about what makes our company unique and special. By now you have found products or services that you love and reasons that you have decided to do this as a business. It's important to really understand what's different about our company because there are other companies out there that do similar things.

You will want to be able to explain to your business builders and customers what it is that makes us different. Knowing what makes us different and special will help you close the deal, present the company more naturally, and help you become trustworthy to others.

- [List out five to seven bullet points that make your company different.]

Now that you know a few things that make our company different, take some time to identify a few more reasons that make our company special. Remember, knowledge is power—the more you know, the more successful you will be.

Have a great week!

[Your team name or your name]

Email 5: *What to Do - Month 2* - Give them step-by-step instructions of what they can be doing in their second month. Focus on activities that will help them see results. Share with them different sections from this book and help them to be creative and try new things to find success.

Example:

Hey!

Hope you had another great week. What did you learn about the company? One of the great things about what we do is the opportunity we have to always learn more. Please feel free to share with us what you have learned and some of the things that make our company special on the Facebook Group.

You're now at the start of month two. How do you feel like your first four weeks went? Take some time to think about the first four weeks, work on things that need to be improved, and continue doing the things that went well. The first four weeks you were focusing on prospecting, creating a list, and talking with people. These steps are important and need to be continuously applied in your business, so remember to do them. This month we are going to focus on a few more things to help take your business to a new level:

1. Continue adding people to your list and contacting them. Remember, these are individuals whom you think would be interested in either being a customer or business builder. Simply reach out to them and let them know what it is you're doing and add value to their life.

2. Start using social media to grow your business. Find yard sale groups, community pages, or other groups and look for people with common connecting points. This could be business owners or people interested in topics related to your product or service. Once you have found groups with common interests, start participating in the group. Add comments to people's posts and create your own posts. Most of the time these posts won't be

about business, but a legitimate way to connect with people. Try to connect with 20-30 new people each week.

3. Continue learning. Take time to learn more and familiarize yourself with the company.

4. Set up two classes. Work with the people on your list that have expressed interest and schedule a time to come and talk to them and a few of their friends. Let us know how we can help with these classes or if you would like us to teach the first one with you.

Apply these four things and you will have a great second month! Get your class scheduled this week and let us know when it is and how we can help you succeed. You're doing great. Keep it up!

Have a great week,

[Your team name or your name]

Email 6: *Compensation Plan - Part 1* - Break down the compensation plan and point out specific ways they can benefit from it the most. Many times people get overwhelmed when they see a compensation plan and it stops them from moving forward. Help them to see, in simple steps, how easy it is to make money with your compensation plan.

Example:

Hey!

It's hard to believe it has been six weeks already since you decided to become a business owner and change your life. You're doing great! By now you're well on your way to growing a successful business. Are you ready for your first class? I bet you're excited, maybe even a bit nervous. That's ok!!! We all were nervous when we started out. Just remember we are here to help you. Your main goal during the class is to add value to the lives of these people and the sale will follow.

This week we will be talking about some of the basic points of our compensation plan. This plan is absolutely one of the best in the industry! We can make great money using the plan when we really understand how it works.

- [List out five to seven facts about the compensation plan, what they mean, and how to benefit from them. This does not need to be super complicated, but be sure to give enough information to help them succeed.]

Take some time this week to really study the principles mentioned above. Understanding the compensation plan is key to the success of your business. Next week we will be looking at the compensation plan even a bit more in depth.

Have a great week!

[Your team name or your name]

208

Email 7: *Compensation Plan - Part 2 -* Take the compensation plan a bit further and break it down even more. Build upon the previous information you shared to help them see the success that can come from understanding the compensation plan in more detail.

Example:

Hey!

I hope your week has gone well and that you have enjoyed learning a bit about the compensation plan.

Today we are going to dive more in depth about this generous compensation plan and ways to really maximize its benefits.

* [List out seven to ten points on the compensation plan and be sure to define them and really help them understand how the compensation plan can make them money. Remember, this needs to be more in depth than last week's email and more of an advanced version of the compensation plan, but still something they can digest.]

I hope you have enjoyed learning a bit more about how we make money and found some ways to maximize the benefits of our compensation plan. Take some time to learn more and really understand the ins and outs of our compensation plan. Let us know what questions you have.

Have a great week!

[Your team name or your name]

Email 8: *Success is Yours—Take It!* - People want to be successful, but many times they forget they can do it. Remind them of their potential, help them see that it can become a reality, and offer your support along the way.

Example:

Hello!

I hope you're having another great week and that you're starting to really see success from your business. How do you feel about the compensation plan? Do you feel a bit more prepared to teach it, live it, and make money from it?

This week we will be talking about success and how it is just there waiting for us to take advantage of it. You have been doing the business for almost two months and we are sure you have had some tough spots, hit a few obstacles, and been told no by several people along the way. Guess what? That's all just part of it and sometimes it sucks—but don't let those times stop you.

One of the best things about this industry is that we all have the opportunity to succeed, grow, and be the best at what we do. This is not just something we say to keep you going, but something we truly believe. When times get hard remember to focus on what made you get started, your "why", and your motivation to keep going. Remember, we are here as a team to support and help you. You really can do this. Success is there for you, so decide today to take it and don't let anyone tell you otherwise.

Have a great week and keep working! You got this!!!

[Your team name or your name]

Email 9: *What to Do - Month 3* - Give them step-by-step instructions of what they can be doing in their third month. Help them build on previous efforts and share with them different sections from this book to help them to continue to succeed.

Example:

Hey!

Congratulations on your first two full months of business—you're doing great! Keep up the good work and remember like we discussed last week, you can become a huge success. Don't give up, just keep going!

This week we will be giving you a few tips and things to do to help you during your third month in the business.

1. Continue learning. Make a goal to learn something daily and focus on what you need to know. Being knowledgeable on the topic is going to be key to you growing as a leader and building your business.

2. Keep adding people to your list. Find new people and continue to talk with them.

3. Continue connecting with interested people on Facebook. By now you should have been able to meet up or have a phone call with a few of these people and presented the company.

4. Get your team members involved in classes. Teach them what it takes to hold a successful class by showing them what you do in your classes.

5. Continue to teach two to four classes per month.

6. Find three business groups and attend their classes. If there are none in your area, find other types of groups that will allow you to connect with new people.

7. Remember to add value to people's lives and get to know them. We are in the industry of relationships.

8. Commit to completing three to five revenue generating activities (RGA's) daily. (We will explain this in more detail next week)

Get started on these tasks today. Make it an amazing third month. You have so much going for you, so keep going and let us know how we can help.

[Your team name or your name]

> **Tip:** The first 90 days is so important to a new business builder. Be sure to keep them motivated, give them tasks to help them see results, and be there to support them. Try to personally connect with them at least once a month or more frequently if possible. If you can keep them excited, motivated, and seeing results, you will have a much higher chance of having a lifetime business builder.

Email 10: *RGA's* - Teach them about activities they can do on a daily basis to generate volume. New business builders often get overwhelmed and struggle to think of daily things they can do, so make sure to show them simple solutions.

 Reference: Please see the Sales chapter in this book for more details on RGA's.

Example:

Hey!

Hope you have had another successful week! How did it go last week? Did you get started on your third month's task?

This week we are going to talk about something that can really change your business—and if completed on a regular basis, can result in a large increase in your business within a short amount of time. RGA's are crucial and so many times are forgotten.

It is important that before you do anything else in your business each day that you first focus on three to five activities that will generate revenue for your business. This is the best way to grow. So many times we get caught up in creating business cards, working on a website, or other little things that are important, but can get in the way of your success or take up all of your time. So remember to create revenue first and then work on the other projects. You will find a list below of a few RGA's to help you get started:

- Call customers who have not purchased within the last six weeks.

- Send Facebook messages to friends or family members asking them if they know anyone who might be interested in your business.

- Talk to local businesses and find ways to mutually help each other grow.

Just remember the entire goal of these is to increase revenue and make you money. If it does not do that then it is not an RGA. Take time this week to make sure you complete three to five RGA's before you do anything else. Remember, all activities to build your business are important, but this strategy simply puts the best activities first.

Keep working and stay determined. You're doing great! We are here if you need anything. Have a great week!

[Your team name or your name]

> **Tip:** Remember to keep the ideas and suggestions you give them for RGA's simple and productive. When possible provide them with ways that will guarantee an increase in their business. You want RGA's to be something that motivates them and not discourages them about the business.

Email 11: *Leaders* - Teach your team members how to become leaders by giving them the tools they need to lead and support their teams. Identify characteristics of a good leader and teach these to your business builders. Encourage them to focus on their strengths and help them strengthen their weaknesses. Be the leader you want them to become!

> **Reference:** Please see the Leadership chapter in this book to learn more about becoming a successful leader.

Example:

Hey!

What did you think of RGA's? What kind of results have you seen from them? It is amazing that prioritizing them can make such a difference in your business. Keep putting RGA's first, teach them to your team, and enjoy the success that will come from them.

This week we are going to be talking about leadership and the importance of being a leader. Many times people join this industry as a business builder because they are looking for something different than the typical nine-to-five job, some flexibility in their schedule, and the potential that the industry brings. Basically people join because they want freedom! As a leader, our job is to work with our team, help them be a success, and help them see the freedom they can truly have with hard work and dedication.

As a leader, our goal is to be there for our team, support them, and guide them to success. We are in an industry that has so much potential and we are responsible to help our teams get there. Leaders work with their teams and don't expect them to do all the work. They are right there with them working hard, hitting goals, and making things happen. Remember to lead by example. Don't have your team do anything that you would not do yourself.

If you fall short in any of these areas, commit today to change and make improvements. It is important to develop the skill set needed to be an amazing leader and someone your team can rely on for help and support. Get started now!

Keep up the good work and remember we are here to help you. Have a wonderful week!

[Your team name or your name]

> **Tip:** Strive to be the best leader you can be and let them know that you are constantly trying to improve. One of the biggest things that makes leaders great is their ability to constantly improve. Keep at it and help your new business builders see that. By letting them see this constant need to improve it helps them see you're not perfect and they can relate much better with you.

Email 12: *Commit to Succeed* - Show your team that you're committed to becoming a success and helping them become successful too. They need to know that you're there to help them succeed and in it for the long run.

Example:

Hey!

Wow! It's hard to believe you have already been working hard for three months. What a difference you have made on our team. I'm so excited to have been able to work with you so far and to experience the success we've had together! How are you doing on developing your leadership qualities? Remember, being a leader is key to success in the industry. Keep at it!

I want you to know that I'm committed to this business and to your success. I've had the opportunity to work with you and others and have seen the success that comes from this business. You are going to be an amazing leader and contributing member of our team!

Make the choice today to be committed and determined to stick it out to the end. We know it gets hard at times—and that's ok—but keep going. If you stay motivated, work hard, and don't give up, you're going to see huge success.

We're here to support you every step of the way! Have a great week and keep going!

[Your team name or your name]

3. Weekly Business Calls

Weekly business calls can be a great combination of information from both the Facebook Groups and the email campaigns. These calls can be ongoing and used for all business builders at all skill levels. They also provide a great opportunity to help business builders learn from each other and create a unified group. Use this as an opportunity to teach a simple principle, a detail about the business, or something you learned from this book.

 Tip: Give your team copies of this book to help you generate topics for your weekly business calls.

Keep these calls short and productive. I like to limit them to 45 minutes each—setting aside time for instruction, questions, and discussion. This will get your leaders talking and allows others to hear opinions, tactics, and ideas from the group. It will give them ideas that they can implement in their efforts and provide solutions to challenges that they come across.

Start your call on time to show respect for your team's busy lives. Respecting their time will earn you respect as a leader and help you spend the time efficiently. It is important to stay on topic and stick to the schedule. Additionally, you can promote these calls in the footer of each email or post reminders on your Facebook Groups.

Tip: It's important to give your business builders opportunities to get involved. I like to occasionally assign the topic out to a member on the team—either a new or advanced business builder—prior to the call. This is a great opportunity for the business builder to practice teaching and instructing others. It will also help them develop essential skills to become a successful leader.

Here is an example of a call schedule with a brief explanation of how to host and execute your weekly business calls:

8:30-8:35 pm *Start Call* - Make sure to start on time and keep this part lighthearted and fun. Simply welcome your team and get them excited for the call. This time can also be used to follow up on the previous call's invitation.

8:35-8:40 pm *Welcome New Business Builders or Recognition* - Briefly introduce any new business builders or recognize any achievements—this could be rank advancements, enrollments, or anything applicable. Remember, people love to be recognized because it makes them feel important and valued.

8:40-9:00 pm *Educate* - This is the biggest chunk of the call and one of the most important. Teach your team new ideas and help them better understand the business. Be sure to have this planned out—something that is clear to understand and shows your respect for their time.

9:00-9:10 pm *Questions* - Open up the call for questions and discussion. Start by answering questions related to the call's topic and then expand into any other business-related questions. Remember to keep this section on schedule and at the end, remind people to work with their direct uplines to get questions answered in between calls.

9:10-9:15 pm *Invitation and Farewell* - Everything you do needs to have an invitation. Take some time to invite them to apply what you discussed, implement a new strategy, or to talk to a set number of people daily. The invitation needs to be relevant with the education part of the call, and something that helps them progress and move forward. After the invitation, thank them for their time and end the call.

Customers

Now that we have discussed some of the ways to educate your business builders, let's talk about those individuals that use your product or service. These are the people that make your business a success and you'll always want and need more customers. It is important to educate them and continue educating them to create loyal returning customers. You need at least 90% of your organization to be customers and only 10% business builders. Focus on helping them, teaching them, and keeping them happy!

I support my customers in three ways:

1. Facebook Groups

2. Email Campaigns

3. Weekly Product or Service Calls

1. Facebook Groups

These groups are an amazing way to create an exciting and fun atmosphere for your customers, just like the business Facebook Groups. Each person that joins my team, whether planning on building the business or simply using the product, gets added into this group. Use it to teach about your company from a consumer's perspective. Provide incentives and extra opportunities to create loyal and satisfied customers. Posts on this page should be engaging and consistent. Posts should occur twice a day with a minimum of five days per week and one post per day on the weekends.

Follow the weekly schedule listed below for your customers in the education group:

Monday

Post 1: Product or Service Highlight - Teach and educate your customers on the products or services your company offers. Through product education you will help them become loyal to you and the company.

Example Posts:

1. Did you know [product or service] can help you with [benefit] and with [benefit]? Give it a try!

2. Did you know [product or service] is one of [your company name]'s most popular products or services? It was one of the company's first and can bring many benefits into your life! Check it out!

Post 2: Product or Service in Action - Using the product or service from the previous post, demonstrate how to use, implement, and apply it in your life. This is a huge part of this group. You must be able to show your customers not only what it is you offer, but how to use it and really benefit from it.

Example Posts:

1. Have you thought about replacing your everyday household items with some of these amazing products? Use [product] in your kitchen, living room, or even the bathroom. It's a great way to use an amazing product and save some cash!

2. Switching over to using [your company name]'s products or services can be easy. Let us know if you have questions and we will be glad to help in the transition.

Tuesday

Post 1: Company Difference - What makes your company special and different? Why would your customer purchase from you and your company over others?

Example Posts:

1. One of the things that makes [your company name] unique is the amazing quality of the products. Rest assured that you're getting amazing quality at a great price.

2. Unlike other companies, we have been around for [number] years. All these years of experience really make our company stand out. What has been your favorite thing about [company] so far?

Post 2: FAQ's - Take some time and answer common questions that your customers have. This is a great way to get them involved and interacting.

Example Posts:

1. Did you know [insert company fact here]?

2. I am often asked about how to use [product name]. (Then answer the question with a few ideas of how to use the said product or service)

Wednesday

Post 1: Did You Know? - Post fun facts about your products or services. Think of topics that people might not know about or that would get their attention. This post is meant to help them learn more about you and the company, so get creative with it.

Example Post:

1. Did you know [product] can help you [insert benefit]?

Post 2: Fun Fact - Take time to get to know your customers by sharing a bit about yourself, by sharing a fun video, or something similar. Be real. Let them know you're a real person and that there is more to life than just business.

Examples Posts:

1. Today we had the opportunity to visit the local zoo! It was a great day with the family and I was even able to use [product]!

2. This hit my funny bone! Check out this hilarious video. #funny [insert link to a funny, yet appropriate video]

Thursday

Post 1: Personalized Questions - Ask questions to get your customers sharing and discussing how the products or services you offer have personally affected their lives. How have they used this product? How has this service made their life easier? What is their favorite way to use the product? Or simply ask what their favorite product is. This interaction will keep your company's products or services top of mind, build value in the products or services, and help your customers make personal connections about why they matter in their lives.

Example Posts:

1. How do you like [product or service]?

2. What's your favorite [company] product or service to use?

3. How have you benefited from [company]'s product or service?

Post 2: Product or Service Highlight - Follow the same instructions on these sections under Monday's posts.

Friday

Post 1: Inspiration - Use a quote or inspiring video to motivate your customers. This should be simple and not overthought.

Example Post:

1. "Life is 10% what happens to you and 90% how you react to it." - Charles Swindoll

Post 2: Product or Service in Action - Follow the same instructions on Monday's post.

Saturday

Weekend Fun - Wish your customers a happy weekend and give them a few fun tips on how to use your product or service over the weekend. Remember to keep it simple. You want them to have practical ideas to use the product while enjoying the weekend.

Example Post:

1. I hope everyone has had a great week and is excited for the weekend! Take some time and enjoy it with friends and family. Remember to take [product] or [product] with you!

Sunday

Inspiration - Follow the same instructions on these sections under Friday's post.

 Tip: Along with the suggested material for each post, add an engaging photo to enhance the text.

2. Email Campaigns

Customer email campaigns are similar to business email campaigns in the sense that they are meant to teach and go more in depth into a topic. It should help them understand what your company does and how it will benefit them.

Give practical uses when you can to show them how to use what you offer. Use these emails to encourage your customers, to try new items, and to take advantage of promotions. I would recommend writing no less than 24 emails and send them out once a week for 24 weeks.

Let's break down the basic structure of each email. They need to include the following items:

Basic Email Structure

- **Greeting** - Start with a simple welcome. Thank them for their time and remember to keep it short. This does not need to be a huge section in the email, but it is quite important. You want to capture their attention within the first sentence or two so they continue reading the email and get to the good stuff.

- **Last Week Follow Up** - Follow up on the previous week's email by asking a few questions or talking about what you discussed. Say something like, "I hope you enjoyed trying..."

- **Education** - This section should be the bulk of the email, take some time (a paragraph or two) to discuss a new topic and educate them. Teach them how to use it, how to apply it in their life, or how it will benefit them.

- **Invitation** - Invite them to use and apply something you just taught them. This could be to learn more about the topic, to use the product or service, or just a simple invitation.

- **Farewell** - End the email, again thank them for their time, and be sure to leave them excited and ready for next week's communication.

Now that you know how the basic structure of each email should look, let's dive into the topics for the 24 days:

Email 1: *Welcome* - Welcome your customers and thank them for trusting you with their business. Let them know what they can look forward to from these emails and get them excited about being a customer with your company.

Example:

Hello!

Welcome and thank you for becoming one of our valued customers. We are excited to work with you and are here if you have any questions or need anything. Customer service is our main focus so we want you to enjoy your experience.

Over the next several weeks we will be sending you an email with basic information you will need to make purchases, as well as contact information to those who can assist you with questions, information about products or services, or exciting news and facts about this great company.

Personally I have been with the company for five years and can't imagine my life without it! Take some time this week to look at our website and learn more about what [your company name] offers. Remember, we are here if you need anything!

Have a wonderful week!

[Team name or your name]

Email 2: *Support System* - Let them know they have a support system. This is super important! Take time and let them know how to contact you, the company, and anyone else that is important to making sure they have the best customer experience.

Example:

Hey!

I hope you had a wonderful week! How has your experience been with [your company] so far? What do you think? Anything we can do to help you?

This week we will be talking about your support system. One of the great things about companies like [company] is that you have multiple people excited and willing to help you.

- [Your name and number]

- [Your company's customer service phone number and hours of operation]

- [Company's email, chat support, and hours of operation]

- [Your customer Facebook Group, name, and link]

These are several great resources. If you have questions, don't hesitate to ask them. Reach out and let us know how we can help. Write these down and put them in a place where you can reference them easily in a time of need.

Remember, we are here to help you!

Have a great week!

[Team name or your name]

Email 3: *How to Order or Access* - Make sure your customers not only know that you're a support for them, but also be sure they know how to order and access the information they need. It's important that your customers learn to be independent in using the resources made available to them. Don't do everything for them—instead, practice the concept of "teaching a man to fish."

Example:

Hey!

Hope this email finds you well. How are you enjoying these amazing products or services?

Today we are going to be talking about how to order and access information when needed. Below you'll find a list of important items everyone must know:

- *Ordering:* [Give details about what they need to do to order. For some companies this will be logging into a back office and for others it will be a link to purchase from. Be detailed and give them the information they need to order on a regular basis and without having to contact you each time.]

- *Information:* [Give them any extra information, websites, and other things they might need. Don't overwhelm them. However, give them resources that will help them become independent.]

This week login and check the link to make sure everything works. If there are any issues, let us know.

Have a great week!

[Team name or your name]

Email 4: *Embrace the "New"* - Help your customers understand the benefits of using your company's products or services and how these will impact their lives. Help them to embrace the company and become loyal customers.

Example:

Hey!

Hard to believe you have been a customer for four weeks! Now that you know the basics of the company, how do you feel? Any questions we can help answer?

This week we will talk all about embracing your company in your life and what it takes to really make the company a part of you and your family. You will find a few tips below to make this a part of your daily life:

• [Give two to four tips about your company's products or services]

• [Show two to four practical ways to implement the company into their life]

I remember when I started with the company and learned about the benefits of these amazing products or services. It would be hard to imagine life without them! Take time to find some of your favorite products or services and try a few of these tips. Let us know what you think.

Take care!

[Team name or your name]

Email 5: *Promotions and Incentives* - Teach them about the promotions offered to customers and how they can maximize the benefits to get the best deals and offers. This will help your customers trust you and know you have their best interests in mind.

Example:

Hey!

Hope you're having an amazing week! How have you used the products and services this week? What is your favorite part of being involved with [your company]?

Let's dive into some of the great promotions and incentives offered by our team and the company.

- [Share any regular promotions—monthly or weekly ones your company may have and give them the information on how to take advantage of them.]

- [Let them know about any team promotions that take place regularly.]

Take some time and learn a bit more about these great promotions.

Let us know if you have any questions.

[Team name or your name]

Email 6: *Maximizing Benefits* - This email is designed to help the customer understand how to get the most for their money, ways to get free products or services, autoship programs your company may offer, and learn of any program that rewards them for being a loyal customer. Take the time to make sure they understand all of the options available to them.

Example:

Hey!

Hope you had another great week. What did you think about those amazing promotions? It's amazing the benefits the company offers their customers. Don't forget to take advantage of these great deals!

This week we will explain a bit more about some additional programs the company has that can really make a difference and can help you get free or discounted items, participate in reward programs, and so on. Check out some of these great loyalty programs:

• [If your company has an auto ship program and offers rewards for those that purchase regularly, share that here. Give them the details about the program and the value they receive for being involved with this program.]

• [Share with them any other ways your company may offer to help them get free or discounted products or services.]

If you have any questions about these amazing programs, let us know. Don't miss out on an opportunity to get more for your money!

Have a wonderful week!

[Team name or your name]

Email 7 - *Company Difference* - What makes your company special and different? This is important to share with your customers. Let them know why you started with the company and make connections about the good the company can do for them.

Example:

Hey!

I hope you have had time to learn a bit more about the amazing programs the company offers and ways to get additional discounts and even free items.

This week we will be talking a bit more about the company and some of the things that make it different. We are lucky to be involved with a company that truly is different from others.

- [List out five to seven differences that make your company unique. Talk about these and explain why they are important.]

Take some time this week to identify and learn a bit more about what makes our great company different.

Let us know if you have any questions or if there is anything we can do for you.

[Team name or your name]

Emails 8-17 - *Product or Service Highlight* - Teach, teach, and teach some more. Educate your customers on what your company offers. Dive into the details of specific products or services. If your company doesn't have a ton of products or services, explain the one you have in more detail. Remember, you will need to cover nine different emails regarding this.

Example:

Hey!

Another week has gone by and we have really enjoyed getting to know you a bit more. Now that we have discussed the company, some of the differences, and great opportunities for our loyal customers, let's talk about some of the amazing products or services we offer!

This week we will be talking about [choose a specific product or service]. [Provide details about it, what it does, how it can be used, etc. Be sure to give them a good amount of information.]

Try this product or service out! Let us know what you think after trying it out!

Have a great week!

[Team name or your name]

Emails 18-19 - Frequently Asked Questions (*FAQ's*) - What questions do your customers have on a regular basis? Take some time to write these out and provide the answers. Let them know they are not alone and that most people have similar questions.

Example:

Hey!

How have you enjoyed learning about some of our amazing products or services? These are some of the biggest things that make our company different and unique.

This week we are going to talk a bit about FAQ's. Many of our customers have common questions they want answers to. Hopefully these will help you out.

* [List out five to seven FAQ's and give them good answers. Remember, you will be doing this over two emails so disburse the questions out evenly.]

Please read over these and let us know if you have any questions or anything we can do for you.

Have a great week!

[Team name or your name]

Email 20 - *Did You Know? (Business Opportunity)* - This is your chance to present the business opportunity to your customers. Do this in a lighthearted way, letting them know there is an opportunity they can benefit from financially.

Example:

Hey!

Another week has come and gone—time flies! Did the questions help you out? Hopefully they provided some more details for you to understand them better.

This week we want to take a couple minutes and talk about another great aspect of our company. One of the benefits of working with a company like [your company name] is we get to promote a product or service we love and make money while doing it!

It really is amazing they pay us a commission to talk about something we love. Some people do this in a casual, part time way while others use it to see financial success, impact many people, and build a successful business.

Here are a few great benefits of making this a business:

• [List out three to five benefits of making this a business. Remember to keep it simple, lighthearted, and not pushy.]

Think this over and let us know if there is anything we can do. If you're interested in learning more about the business, let us know!

Have a wonderful week!

[Team name or your name]

Email 21 -*Did You Know? (Changing Lives)* - Take time to tell them about the good that comes from your company. This may be a foundation, nonprofit work, or simply the amazing opportunities it provides people to better their lives.

Example:

Hey!

Another week has come and gone. Hopefully you enjoyed last week's email learning a bit more about the amazing benefits of creating a successful business with [your company name].

One of the other things that makes [your company name] so special is the amazing way they give back!

• [List out three to five things your company does to give back. Give details about what they do and the good they do in the world.]

It's amazing to be involved with a company that is so great to us, but also gives back to so many! What an amazing opportunity we have. Try to do something this week to give back to someone else!

Have a great week!

[Team name or your name]

Email 22 - *Now What?* - Take a few minutes and give them some exciting news, next steps, and an explanation on how to continue using your products or services. This is a great opportunity to make sure they have everything they need to continue as a loyal customer.

Example:

Hey!

How did giving back go last week? Have you had a chance to get involved? What an amazing opportunity it is to give back to people around us and make life a bit better for someone else.

This week we will take a few minutes to give you a few additional pointers, some upcoming classes and news, and other aspects that will benefit you!

• [List out five to seven things they might need to know about such as new promotions, exciting classes, and much more. Keep it simple, don't overwhelm them, and add value.]

Look these over and let us know if you're interested in learning more about any of them.

Have a great week!

[Team name or your name]

Email 23 - *We Appreciate You!* - Take time to thank them for being loyal customers and express appreciation for their involvement in your company.

Example:

Hey!

Hopefully you found last week's email interesting and beneficial.

This week we want to take just a minute to say thank you! We are so glad to be working with you and to have you as a loyal customer. Almost six months ago, we started working together and we truly appreciate your business. We value you, our friendship, and the great opportunity we have to work together.

If there is anything we can do differently or to improve your experience we would love to hear from you!

Have a great week and thanks again for being so great!

[Team name or your name]

Email 24 - *We're Excited to Work with You and We're Here to Support You* - This is the final email, but it is important to let them know you're there for them and want to help them if they ever need anything.

Example:

Hey!

I wanted to thank you one more time for your loyalty and for being one of our valued customers.

This is the last email of our customer education emails. We wanted to reach out and let you know that we are here for you. If there is anything that you need, please don't hesitate to contact us. If you decide in the near future you are interested in the business opportunity, please let us know and we will be glad to help you get started.

Over the last few weeks we have had an amazing opportunity to get to know you, tell you a bit more about some of the great things the company does, and how it can benefit all of us.

Thanks again! Looking forward to connecting with you soon.

[Team name or your name]

3. Weekly Education Calls

I look forward to my weekly customer calls and seriously believe these are a total blast! I love getting on a call and really just talking about why I love the company that I am with and what it has done for me and my life. Remember to keep these calls on schedule and make sure they are professional, but lighthearted.

You want your customers to see you as someone who is a respectful business person. When you first start, your customers may include some of your friends and family—and that is ok! Still be professional and focused because you're setting your team up for success and growth. You might be surprised by how quickly your team could expand. Make sure that each call has an invitation to act or invitation to take action. You'll want to have this planned out ahead of time because it will give direction and purpose to your calls.

Here is an example with a brief explanation of how to host and execute your weekly customer call:

8:30-8:35 pm *Start Call* - Make sure to start on time. Keep this part lighthearted and fun. Simply welcome your customers and get them excited for the call. This time can also be used to follow up on the invitation from the previous call.

8:35-8:40 pm *Product Promotions* - Talk about fun promotions the company or your team is having and how these promotions can be used. Or discuss fun facts about the company.

8:40-9:00 pm *Educate* - This is the biggest chunk of the call and one of the most important. Teach your customers new ideas, new ways of using the products or services, and how to implement them in their lives. Be sure to have this planned out. It needs to be something that is clear to understand and shows that you respect their time.

9:00-9:10 pm *Questions* - Open up the call for questions and discussion. Start by answering questions related to the call's topic and then expand into any other topics.

9:10-9:15 pm *Invitation and Farewell* - Everything you do needs to have a call to action or an invitation. Take some time to invite them to apply what you discussed, to try a new product or service (when applicable), or to just do something that gets them progressing. After the invitation, thank them for their time and end the call.

We have covered a lot of information in this chapter. Take time to let it sink in and read it over a few times. It's ok to start small and implement different portions as your business grows. Be committed to educate your team and be there to support them.

To Do List

☐ Pick three items to educate yourself on and master them

☐ Identify three to five differences between your company and your its competitors

☐ Identify who is a business builder and who is a customer on your team

☐ Create Facebook Groups

☐ Write business emails

☐ Create posts for groups

☐ Create business and customer emails

 Tip: To learn more, follow me at facebook.com/ trainwithjustin

Chapter Notes

Chapter 7
Leadership

When asked what one of the most important areas someone should work on to become successful in the industry is, I always respond—without hesitation—to become a trusted and successful leader! Being a great leader separates the successful from the posers, it's what allows people to grow million-dollar organizations, and it's what drives people to experience success at the summit. People want to follow a leader who motivates, encourages, and inspires them to become better.

In this chapter, we will discuss some tactics and ways that you can become the best leader possible and to help others do the same. Let's get started!

Qualities of an Effective Leader

Take a moment to think about the different leaders that have had a positive impact on or made a difference in your life. These individuals could be a parent, a teacher, a religious leader, a friend, a colleague, a manager, a coach, a neighbor, or any number of other influential people. Great leaders come from all different backgrounds and possess different qualities that make them exceptional.

I can think of many different individuals whom I consider to be amazing leaders in my life. I remember one particular individual that I knew while I was living in Costa Rica. He had no idea what he was doing within his business, nor did he really understand his real potential. However, he showed up everyday ready to work hard, ready to learn, and willing to help others feel important. I will never forget the day he gave his first class.

He was nervous and shaking, but he stood tall, excited to be there, and shared his genuine passion about what motivated him to succeed. I have never been so motivated to act as I was that day! He connected with me on a deeper level, which made me forget about his imperfections. At this point I came to realize that leaders come from all different walks of life and there is so much more to being a leader than what you might typically think. Being a successful leader is less about what you know and more about how you make others feel about themselves, how you motivate them to succeed, and your ability to let others know you're there to support them in times of need.

Think about why specific individuals were great leaders in your life. It could be because they were very knowledgeable about a certain topic and shared that with you, or they were confident in themselves and their efforts, or they connected with you on a personal level, or a variety of other reasons. Great leaders inspire those that they lead and in a business sense, this can empower teams to be confident, prepared, and effective in their efforts.

> **Tip:** Take time to identify several leaders in your life. What made them great leaders? What did you learn from them? How did they impact your life? Now that you have identified the qualities that made these leaders great, be sure to share these experiences with your team when the time is appropriate.

The goal of this section is to help you see the importance of leadership, identify characteristics of leaders, develop the needed skills to become the leader you should be, and to help others do the same. There are many different qualities that make leaders great. I have recognized a pattern of ten qualities that I have seen in great leaders that have helped them motivate, inspire, and shape others into better individuals. These include:

1. **Patience** - This may seem like one of the most simple and easy qualities to develop, but from a personal perspective, this can be one of the hardest qualities to master. Patience can be quite hard to have all the time, especially working in an industry of building relationships, growing a team, and working so closely with others. However, as a leader, patience is imperative to practice and develop.

   Patience shows love and understanding, it allows people to feel comfortable working with you, and helps people know that they can come to you for support, on even the dumbest of questions. We all learn concepts and tactics at different speeds.

It's important to recognize this and be encouraging to those that might not comprehend right away. Patience will help individuals become successful over time.

> **Tip:** When you feel like your patience is getting short, take a break. Take some time for yourself and recharge. It is not possible to be patient all of the time, but it is a must as a leader. Take the time needed for a brief break when needed.

2. **Humility** - Great leaders shouldn't need to crave attention or recognition for doing something. They recognize that success comes from not only their personal efforts, but also from the efforts of their team and others. Humble leaders are there to help the team, to work with them when times get tough, and they are able to admit when they are wrong.

3. **Constantly Improving** - A great leader recognizes that we all have room to improve. Just because you hit a certain rank or accomplish a certain task does not mean you should stop improving. Leaders strive to make themselves better constantly and help others do the same. An organization that is continually improving will see success.

> **Tip:** Help your business builders avoid complacency. It's important for them to stay focused and not get too comfortable in one spot. You want to help motivate, teach, and instruct them on how to take the next steps and keep them moving forward.

4. **Lead by Example** - Great leaders never ask their team to do something that they're not willing to do. If you're wanting your team to teach, then you need to be teaching. If you're wanting your team to enroll prospects, then you need to enroll prospects.

If you want them to become better at prospecting, then you need to be there with them not only doing the same thing, but being the best at it. When your team looks to you and knows you're doing the same tasks alongside them, it will motivate them to succeed and the entire team will do better together.

> **Tip:** Show others that you lead by example. You want your business builders to be able to duplicate this quality and help their teams to grow.

5. **Passionate** - Great leaders let their passion, dedication, and love for what they do show. Your team, prospects, and others you come in contact with need to see this. Being passionate means you love your company, you're excited to be doing the work it takes to become a success, and you help others get there.

> **Tip:** Remember to be genuine when you express your passion. Don't fake something that's not real. People can see through insincerity and they can pick up on when you're not being genuine. It's better to be a bit less passionate than to not be sincere and genuine.

6. **Confidence** - Great leaders are confident in themselves and their efforts—they also promote confidence in those they lead. Typically confidence comes from having knowledge and experience about your company. Many people think confidence and humility can't be a part of the same person, however, this is not the case. Being confident does not mean you have to know everything or act like you do. It simply means you're secure with what you do know, and secure with your ability to help and benefit others. Confidence creates a sense of security and at some point your team will need to rely on *your* confidence for them to be a success.

7. **Team Player** - Great leaders realize that there is no "I" in "Team". They work hand in hand with their team to produce results. This should go without saying, but sadly there are so many people within the industry that don't feel like they have a team to support them. Create ways to support your team, to be there for them, and to help them succeed. Use words like "we" instead of "I" and teach them to do the same. Help them to understand you're there to support and help them as are the others on the team.

> **Tip:** Make sure you actually support your team when you say you will. It will be counterproductive if you only offer lip service and don't actually deliver on your words. When the rubber meets the road, you must deliver on your good intentions. This will also establish and strengthen trust between you and your team. Support your team, but also don't do everything for them.

8. **Clear Communicator** - Great leaders understand how to communicate clearly and help others understand what it is they are saying. Being able to teach, motivate, and educate in a way that encourages others and gets them to act is what's needed for success. At times you will need to deliver messages that may not always be welcomed or the easiest to deliver. However, some things just need to be said. Being able to communicate these topics in a way that does not upset or defeat the person is key. Remember to be real and authentic when communicating.

> **Tip:** Ask some of your closest friends and family members if you communicate clearly—and be open to their answers. Do you say exactly what should be said? Are you passive in your approach? Do you hint around things without directly saying them? Are you tactful? Take their answers and set goals to communicate more clearly.

9. **Focused** - Great leaders are focused on the most important items to grow their business and help their team do the same. Many times people get caught up in team drama or things they can't control and this ultimately will stop you from being successful and growing a business. It's important to let hard times, challenging team members, or anything else you can't control roll off your back so you can move forward.

> **Tip:** Try not to take anything personal when dealing with challenging customers or business builders. Listen to them, help them, apologize for their frustrations, and fix things when needed. However, don't be a pushover by doing whatever they say. Stand up for yourself, your team, and your company.

10. **Compassion** - Understand where people are coming from, try to relate with them, and really try to connect with them. Take time to care for them—not only in the business, but also in their life. Take interest in things that are important to them, share experiences with them, and be there for them when they need you.

Obviously there are other qualities that great leaders possess, but this is a sure foundation to have. When you have identified the qualities of a great leader, it is important for you to develop those skills yourself. Have you ever thought about yourself as a leader? Do you really know the importance of being a leader—an individual others will follow and look to for support and guidance? Some of you might think that you can't become a great leader, but that is simply not true. You can develop these qualities, which will help not only your business, but also the lives and businesses of others. So how do you develop these skills and qualities?

Identifying and Developing Personal Leadership Qualities

Now that we have discussed some qualities that great leaders possess, let's talk about developing the skills needed to become this type of leader. If one of your goals is to have a successful business then it is crucial for you to become a great leader in the industry. We are all at different levels of mastery with these qualities and we constantly need to be developing ourselves and improving. Before developing yourself as a leader it is important to identify your strengths and weaknesses. By taking the self evaluation test below, you will be able to identify the exact areas you thrive in and others where improvement might be needed.

Rate yourself on the qualities listed below (1 being the worst and 10 being the best):

	Poor									Excellent
Patience	1	2	3	4	5	6	7	8	9	10
Humility	1	2	3	4	5	6	7	8	9	10
Constant Improvement	1	2	3	4	5	6	7	8	9	10
Lead By Example	1	2	3	4	5	6	7	8	9	10
Passionate	1	2	3	4	5	6	7	8	9	10
Confidence	1	2	3	4	5	6	7	8	9	10
Teamwork	1	2	3	4	5	6	7	8	9	10
Clear Communicator	1	2	3	4	5	6	7	8	9	10
Focused	1	2	3	4	5	6	7	8	9	10
Compassionate	1	2	3	4	5	6	7	8	9	10

Grading Rubric

1-3 If you graded yourself in this range then this is a clear indication that you could use more development in this specific area. Don't beat yourself up, this is a great starting point to becoming a better leader.

4-7 If you graded yourself in this range then it means that you're on the right path, but you have some room for improvement. Keep giving some love to these qualities and stay focused on constantly improving.

8-10 If you graded yourself in this range then you are well on your way to becoming an excellent leader! Continue to develop these qualities and teach and encourage others to do the same.

Tip: Once you've completed your self evaluation test, try giving this same test to a few of your business builders or others that are close to you. Have them fill it out in relation to your own leadership skills and qualities. Sometimes others see things differently from how we see things ourselves.

Having input from others will give you better insight into areas you excel at and ones where improvement might be needed. A word of advice—ask those that take this test to be completely honest in their assessment and don't be offended with the results. You want to become the best leader possible, and to do so you'll need an honest assessment about where you currently stand.

Take this self evaluation test as often as needed. I highly suggest taking it at least monthly to help you keep track of your improvements and to constantly be progressing.

Now that you have identified personal qualities that you need to improve on, it's time to develop these into your strengths. Developing these qualities does not happen overnight, so be patient with yourself. The steps listed below will help you develop the qualities and skills needed to become an excellent leader:

- **Research** - Take time to research the qualities you're trying to improve on and create set plans to make them happen. You could read about these qualities or ask others that you admire to discuss their thoughts about them. Oftentimes we can gain different perspectives from others that will help our understanding of a particular topic grow.

- **Observe and Emulate Others** - Another way you can develop leadership qualities is to find someone that excels in the areas that you are struggling with and observe their approach to them. Ask them how they developed these qualities and write down notes for yourself to review later.

- **Set Goals** - Once you have researched and talked with others, it's time to set goals. Set goals that will hold you accountable and help you grow—but make sure they'll also be attainable. Goals should be something that motivate you to become better and give you a clear path to make it happen. Find someone close to you and share your goals with them. It's important to also write down clear, actionable items that will help you accomplish your goals. Try listing three to five action items for each goal.

- **Practice** - Now that you have set goals, it's time to put those into practice. Oftentimes this can be one of the most difficult parts of developing what's needed to become a leader because it requires you to get out of your comfort zone. Take your goals and action items and work towards them both each day. Keep in mind that no matter how hard you try, there will be days that will be harder than others. Don't let that stop you, keep going.

- **Reevaluate** - It's important to not only set goals and action items, but to reevaluate them on a regular basis. Reevaluate your goals at least monthly or more frequently when needed. This is the most important step to developing the qualities needed to become a successful leader. As you implement these steps, you may be surprised by how quickly you see progress.

> **Tip:** Teach your team the importance of constant improvement and self development. This should be equally as important as increasing volume or finding a new prospect.

Training Others to Become Great Leaders

As you personally improve and develop yourself to become a great leader, it is important to teach others to become great leaders too. Even if you're not perfect, you need to see yourself as someone who can lead others and help them achieve their goals. As discussed previously, it is important to lead by example, and helping others to become great leaders is a part of that. Once you become a leader, your main responsibility becomes helping others to become leaders and to be successful. As they become great leaders, this will help accelerate the success of your efforts because they will be sharing the workload. They'll be implementing the same tactics you've learned, which will complement your efforts and together your business will grow.

3x3 Leadership Development Program

Start developing leaders today with this 3x3 Leadership Development Program. This program is designed to help you be seen as a leader—someone who knows their stuff and can help the team—but it mainly focuses on you teaching others the things they need to do to become leaders and grow their business. Oh, and did I mention it will also increase your volume and new signups?!? It's a win-win and an absolute must for your business. This program consists of selecting three of your business builders or potential leaders and focuses on helping them over a period of 30 days. Follow the steps below to help you get started:

- **Seek** - Take time to really think about your team and be selective who you work with. The individuals that you work with should be eager to grow their business and become leaders, not just someone who will say "yes" all of the time. They need to be committed and ready to work. Each month communicate with your team that you are looking for new business builders to be in your leadership mentor program and see who is interested. Be direct with your communication and make it clear that this program will take work and you want to work with those that are serious about making things happen. If they can't be serious now, that's ok. When the timing is correct for them, you will be there to help them.

Most of the time I communicate this on my Facebook business builder groups, and within a short amount of time, have a great amount of interest. However, you can communicate with your business builders in whatever way works best for you. If you're just getting started and don't have three business builders yet, that's ok. Reach out to those you do have and help them grow. If you don't have interest from them, just be patient and keep promoting it monthly. It's better to be patient and work with those that are ready to become leaders rather than taking someone on just to add body count.

A typical post or communication may look like something like this:

"I am working hard this month to hit some big goals and make things happen and I am looking for three business builders who are ready to get serious and take their business to the next level. If this is you, let me know and let's get your business growing. If you are not ready to work and make a change, then the time might not be right for you. Serious business builders only!"

I want this post to get their attention and to attract those that want to grow their business, become a legitimate leader, and make a difference—and I want it to irritate those who are on the fence. I want it to be just enough of a push to get them to consider whether or not they are ready to do this. I want it to motivate and cause them to do a self evaluation to see if they are really ready to take action. Be kind and understanding to those who can't participate, but stand strong and take on only those that are able and ready to make things happen.

- **Commit and Act** - Once I have generated interest and gotten business builders excited about the leadership development program, I reach out to each one that has expressed interest. Remember, you are only going to select three individuals whom you will qualify and ensure they are really serious about being a success. When you contact each of them, you're going to set some expectations and guidelines with them. Keep in mind you want to keep it short, to the point, and focused on business. This is typically how my calls go:

"Hey John! I am so excited that you are ready to grow your business and take things to the next level—and I am really excited to work with you! Before we get started the first of next month, I just wanted to make sure we were on the same page and make sure this is something you really are going to succeed at. I will be selecting three business builders to spend a good amount of my time training over the next 30 days and I want to make sure you're going to benefit from it. I will need you to be able to work at least ten hours a week on your business—ten uninterrupted hours—where you can focus on your business and nothing else.

I will also need you to set up three phone calls a week with your prospects. This could be friends, family, or anyone you know that might be interested in hearing more about our company. Once you set these up, please let me know and we will do a quick conference call with them. If you can just introduce us, I will take the call from there. [This is when you will train and show them how to present your company to someone, educate on your company's product, service, or opportunity, and invite them to act. Be confident and passionate, and you will be a huge success—you got this!]

Finally, I will need you to set up at least three classes in the month and contact ten people weekly to invite to your classes. [These can be online or in-person. There are pros and cons to both, so decide what works for both of you. Remember, you will be the one teaching at these classes and showing your business builders how to do this. You should teach the first class, the second you should do together, and the third you should be there for support. During the third class, your job is to help when needed, but let them do the bulk of the training and educating.] *So John, now that we have discussed the plan, how does it sound? Seem like something you're ready to do?"*

These are the guidelines and there are no excuses or other options. If they want to do it then move forward and get started. If they give you a reason they can't or they are not comfortable with something simply say, *"I understand that the timing may not be best for you at the moment. I truly know this will change your business, so when you are able to commit to this, let me know and we will get you started. In the meantime, let me know what I can do to help you."*

This may seem rude to some, but that is not the goal. As a leader you need to be seen as someone who knows what's going on and someone who can make things happen. If you're going to help business builders grow their business they need to be working, and this will give them solid steps to succeed. Stay strong and stick to the outlined program—don't allow for excuses. I promise when you tell someone the time might not be right they will quickly change their tone and get ready to work if they truly want to succeed. It will also weed out those who are not really interested or those that just say "yes", but don't act on it. Commit to this and you will see results!

- **Duplicate-** This is the most important part of this entire leadership development program. Now that you have worked with these three business builders for 30 days, it is time for them to become the instructor and do the same activity for their team. They now repeat the exact same process with business builders on their team—you have begun to implement a system that will continue to develop solid leaders, build good habits, and increase overall volume, which will grow your business! Repeat this monthly and once you can handle more than three business builders, scale up to five per month at most. You want to be able to help them succeed and maximize results, so don't overwhelm yourself. Stick to this program and you will have an organization of solid, successful leaders.

> **Tip:** During the 30 days, try to have regular contact with your team. I try to have contact at least daily in one way or another to make sure they have everything they need to succeed.

Within a few months you will have an organization of solid leaders working together to grow a successful business—this is an absolute game changer. Your team will become unstoppable and one of your company's top teams. Be proud of your leadership qualities, be proud of your team, and keep going!

Recognition

One of the biggest responsibilities you have as a leader is to motivate, encourage, and help your team be successful. There are hundreds of ways you can motivate and help your team succeed, but incentives and recognition are going to give you quick results and really help your business builders feel important, needed, and excited to be on your team. Understand when I talk about incentives it doesn't mean you have to spend a huge amount of money or time on something to motivate them. Even the smallest recognition or incentive can drive huge results.

Over the next few pages we will be discussing several ways you can recognize and motivate your team. If you take anything from this section, remember that the smallest and simplest things go a long way. The goal of recognition is nothing more than making people feel good about what they are doing and to let them know they are appreciated. An appreciated leader is a leader that will work hard and be committed to helping you grow your organization. Start this now! Don't wait until you hit a certain rank or a spot in your business. Really help them feel appreciated—even if this is a small card in the mail, a simple text message, or by recognizing them on one of your Facebook business builder groups. Use the list below for creative ideas to help better recognize your business builders.

Tip: Remember to include recognition items in the budgeting step of your Marketing Plan. Keeping track of this will make sure you don't go overboard and stay on budget.

Reference: Please see the Marketing chapter in this book for more information on creating a budget.

- **Birthdays** - Take a quick minute and send your team members a birthday wish. This may seem inconsequential, but it's something that will make a huge difference and impact. If you have the budget for it, get them a small gift and card. Send it to them in the mail, something simple, even if it is a two or three dollar gift, just something for them to open and get excited about. Write a short message wishing them a happy birthday and thanking them for all their hard work. Let them know they are appreciated. If you don't have the budget for a gift, don't let that stop you from simply sending them a card in the mail. In addition to what you send them, take time to make a phone call to wish them a quick happy birthday.

- **New Years** - This is a great opportunity to focus on a "new you" theme. So many people set goals and get excited about the new year. Simply wish them a happy new year, thank them for what they have done, share your goals, and ask them about their goals. Help them see that with the optimism of the new year, there is nothing they can't do.

- **Mother's Day and Father's Day** - Take time to recognize the hard work these individuals do as parents and thank them for their commitment—finding balance as a parent and a business owner is no easy task. Let them know you see the sacrifice they make and how much you appreciate it. These messages can really have a huge impact on your team.

- **Christmas** - If they celebrate this holiday, simply recognize their efforts over the year and send them a quick Christmas card and gift.

> **Tip:** Take into consideration other's personal and religious beliefs. Not everyone celebrates holidays or the holidays that you may celebrate. Being cognizant of other's beliefs will help you determine the best course of action here and help you gain confidence and trust instead of offending others.

- **Firsts** - This is an absolute must. Make it a priority to recognize someone for their first sign up, their first customer, their first class hosted, their first class taught, and so on. Anytime they do something for the first time, recognize them for it and continue to motivate them to do more. This really helps excite your business builders and will help them feel like what they are doing is working. This makes a huge difference and is so crucial! If you only can make one of these ideas work as you get started, it needs to be this one.

- **Milestone Advancements** - Focus on major accomplishments someone has done. Recognize them if they make a rank in record time, earn a high ranking, enroll a crazy amount of prospects, or any number of other amazing accomplishments. If they feel like their hard work has been noticed, they will continue to push to make these types of things happen on a regular basis.

 Tip: Whenever possible, try to publicly recognize people so when others see it, they get excited and motivated too.

Put these ideas into practice! Recognize your business builders, help them feel motivated, and you'll see huge results!

As you focus on developing yourself as a leader, and help others to become great leaders, not only will your business explode, but you will also establish great momentum in your team! Make leadership a priority and constantly strive to be there to support your team at all times. Revisit this chapter from time to time to see where you can improve— after all, you and your business will only benefit from your constant efforts to become better. You won't regret it!

Tip: Oftentimes, others join this industry because they want freedom, they want to see success, and they don't want to have a boss! Keep in mind as a leader, your job is to help them and support them, not to boss them around or treat them like an employee.

Keep these points in mind when comparing what it means to be a leader vs. a boss:

- Bosses use words like "I" and "me". Leaders use words like "we" and "us".

- Bosses go home and expect the team to work and make them successful. Leaders work to help the team grow and realize success will come from working together.

- Bosses try to place blame on others when a problem occurs. Leaders help resolve problems and don't necessarily care what caused it.

- Leaders use encouragement and kindness to motivate and support, whereas bosses motivate with fear.

- Leaders help create an environment where everyone has an equal chance at succeeding while bosses just care about winning and don't care how dishonest or cutthroat it gets.

Be a leader and not a boss.

To Do List

- ☐ Identify three to five leaders that have impacted your life

- ☐ Complete the self evaluation test

- ☐ Research about the qualities you want to improve upon

- ☐ Set goals to improve these qualities

- ☐ Practice becoming better

- ☐ Identify three leaders for the 3x3 Leadership Development Program

- ☐ Find three ways to recognize your business builders for their

  accomplishments or ways to make them feel special

Tip: To learn more, follow me at facebook.com/
trainwithjustin

Chapter Notes

Conclusion

Thank you for joining me on this journey to the summit. We've covered an ample amount of material meant to equip you with the tools you need to reach your goals. Keep in mind that I don't expect you to implement and master everything in this book overnight. You can and should revisit each chapter often to continuously develop yourself and give you ideas of how to help your team experience success. However, the sooner you can start implementing the material in this book, the sooner you will start seeing results from your efforts.

Unlike other books out there, this one provides the exact steps you need to implement to get your business started, to create systems to educate and support your team, and to find new prospects who will implement your company into their lives. Use this book and the corresponding booklet to not only learn, but to master the concepts presented. Share these resources with your team and help them get started on implementing the concepts and tactics taught within—and start growing together.

Remember the analogy of the summit—many dream about reaching the tops of magnificent peaks to take in the majestic vistas, to experience the rewarding feeling that they made it to the top, and to celebrate the lifetime achievement with others. However, very few actually make it to the summit of success simply because they don't have the tools and means to get there. Don't let this become your story.

After reading this book, you cannot use this excuse anymore. I have provided you with step-by-step guidelines, tactics, examples, and tips that will give you the tools you need to scale your proverbial mountain. I believe in you! You can do this! I believe you can become even more successful than you could imagine! We are in an industry with limitless opportunities. Take what's yours and accomplish your dreams.

Most of all, remember to believe in yourself, set your goals, stay focused, work hard, and you will see results. Oftentimes we stand in our own way and stop ourselves from becoming a success. As long as you're committed, you will see success and you will be able to make your dreams a reality. When times get tough take a brief break and get back to it!

Just because you're at the end of the book does not mean this has to be the end of us working together. For more training tips and to stay current with my methods, follow me at **facebook.com/trainwithjustin**. Reach out to me if there is anything I can help you with and remember, I am rooting for you! You have worked hard and your time for success is now. See you at the top!!!

Hope for Honduran Children Foundation

One of the great things about the industry that we work in is the ability to give back and help others live a better and happier life. As I have had the opportunity to travel the world, I have had the privilege of visiting many great countries and regions—South and Central America have always been some of my all-time favorite regions. There are many things that make these countries amazing, but the people are really what makes them special. I have never had the opportunity to work with such humble, kind, and amazing people as I have during my times in South and Central America.

When I started in the industry, I made a commitment to constantly give back and help others succeed and do my very best to live my "why" from day one. Because of my commitment to live my "why" and my love for South and Central America, a portion of each book purchase will be donated to The Hope for Honduran Children Foundation and the Noreen Macbean Training Center. You'll find some information below about this amazing organization and how they work to support the youth of Honduras.

About The Hope for Honduran Children Foundation

The Hope for Honduran Children Foundation is a 501(c)(3) organization dedicated to providing education and housing to orphaned and abandoned boys in one of the most disadvantaged countries in the world. The Foundation works to protect, serve, educate and mentor neglected youth, providing them the knowledge and skills that will enable them to support themselves and improve their villages.

The Noreen Macbean Training Center recently opened its doors and the first classes started in February 2017. After three short months, due to the success of the training center, they had to move to a more modern and larger facility to accommodate the growth and success. The new facility is a short five-minute walk from the Casa Noble transition home operated by the Hope for Honduran Children Foundation. The Casa

Noble home provides underprivileged teenage boys from small, rural villages a chance for a high school education, music and English classes, and prepares them to move on to productive adult lives. The Noreen Macbean Training Center will become an integral part in teaching the boys marketable skills that they will need after high school in order to provide for themselves and their families.

Beautiful, vibrant Noreen Macbean had an enormous passion for life, children, and adventure. She left this life much too early in March of 2015 at the age of 37 in a tragic cycling accident while riding with her cycling club. Noreen loved children, and although she was not able to have any children of her own, she spent countless hours throughout her life working with children and youth, and loved every minute of it. Before her passing, the young girls in the neighborhood would often run to see her as she arrived home from work. She would listen as they told her about their day and laugh as she watched their impromptu gymnastics demonstrations on the front lawn. To Noreen, the children in the neighborhood and the youth she volunteered with became the children she could never have.

Her husband, Allen, along with other family members chose to honor her memory by creating the Noreen Macbean Training Center in Santa Lucia, Honduras. In conjunction with the Hope for Honduran Children Foundation, the Center will provide much needed space, instruction, and equipment to train Honduran youth in micro-enterprises such as sewing, jewelry design, woodcarving, music, and website design.

The first subject offered at the Training Center is sewing, and there will be three classes of five boys each. Some equipment has already been purchased, including basic learning sewing machines, a serger, and a commercial grade sewing machine. An experienced instructor has been hired, and the first project is learning to make the school uniforms all

Honduran children are required to wear. More funding is necessary in order to fully equip the sewing center and ensure its long-term viability. The lessons learned from opening the sewing center will then be applied to the other micro-enterprises that will be taught in the Center as it expands. Entrepreneurial business marketing skills tailored to the Central American business climate will also be offered to maximize the success of the students after finishing their courses. The Center has a goal to become largely self-funding within three to five years through the sale of the goods and services taught in the Center.

With your purchase we will help make dreams a reality. Thank you for being involved with this amazing cause, for helping contribute to my "why", and for making a difference in the world!

For more information visit:

hopeforhonduranchildren.org

Notes

For more information, follow me at

facebook.com/trainwithjustin

45021580R00168

Made in the USA
Middletown, DE
22 June 2017